Coloring Meditation Book for Adult

Stress Relief and Self-Exploration

GongSeon

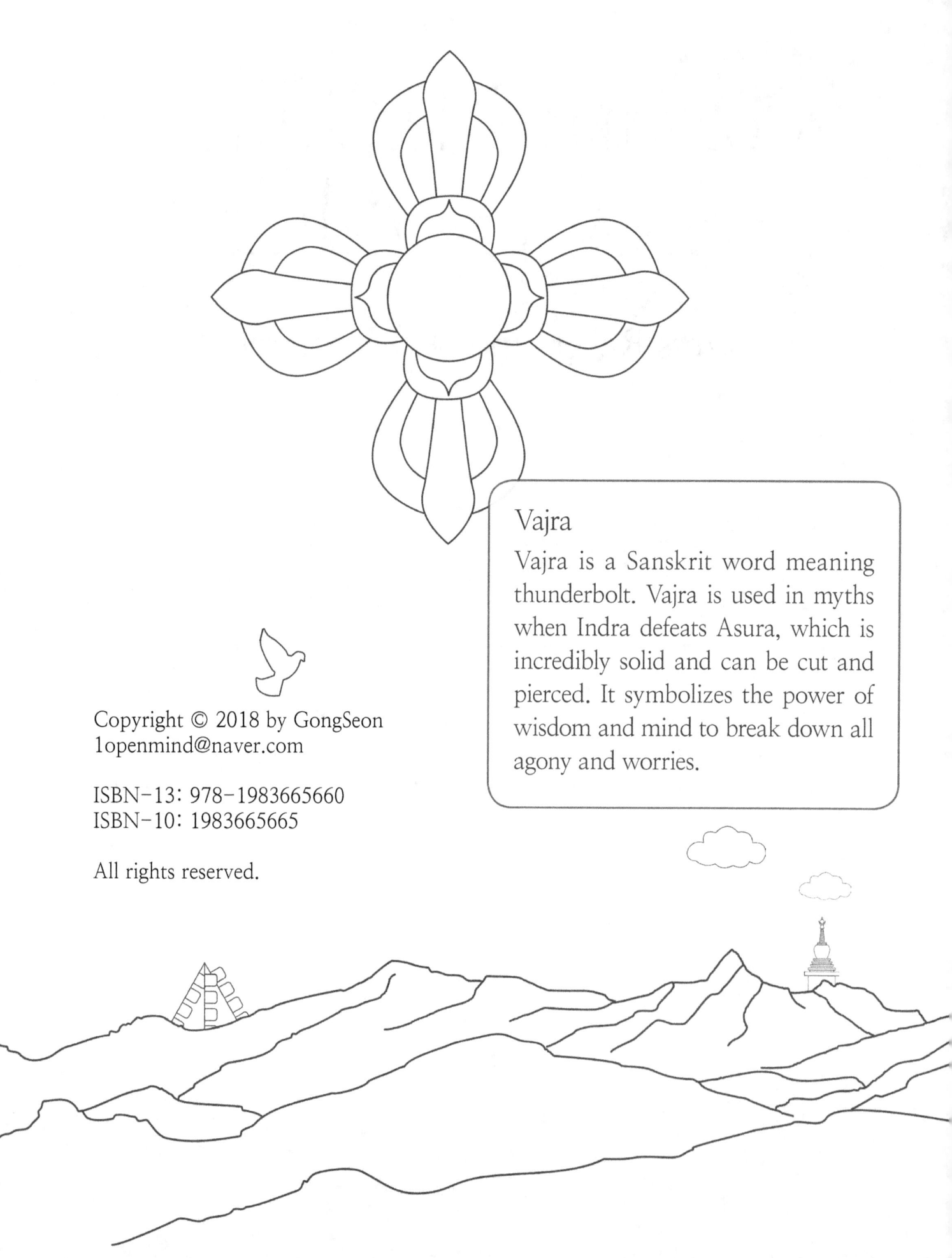

Vajra

Vajra is a Sanskrit word meaning thunderbolt. Vajra is used in myths when Indra defeats Asura, which is incredibly solid and can be cut and pierced. It symbolizes the power of wisdom and mind to break down all agony and worries.

ISBN-13: 978-1983665660
ISBN-10: 1983665665

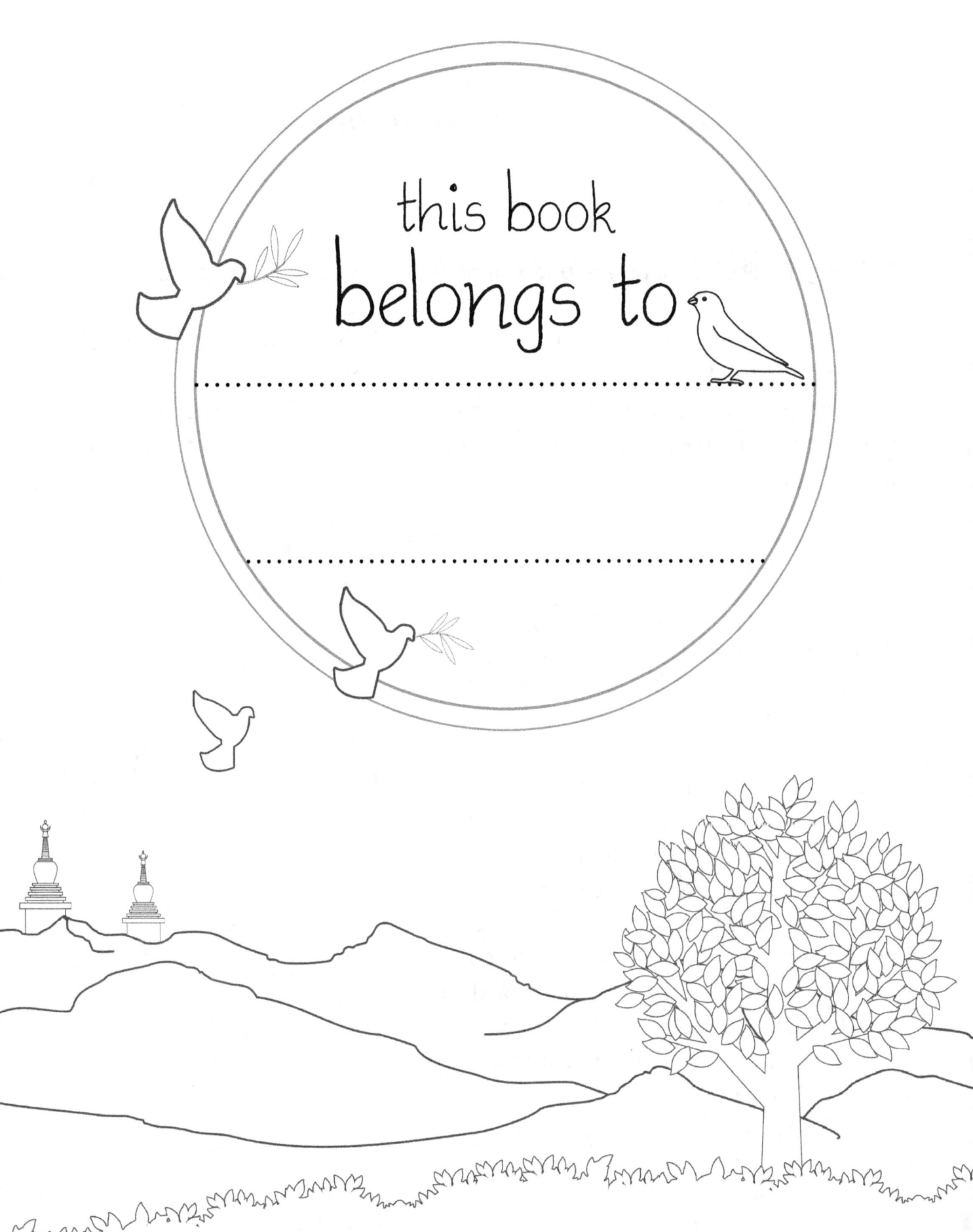

this book
belongs to

Coloring is meditation

Coloring meditation helps you understand the current situation more deeply.

Anyone can simply enter into a state of concentration and comfort through coloring of beautiful, balanced designs. This is one of the form meditations that concentrate on shape or color. By concentrating on the color or shape naturally in the course of coloring the design, the process will soon have the same effect as meditation.

※ Do not have to make efforts to concentrate, because you will concentrate naturally in the process of coloring.

People get stressed as they live. If there is a lot of stimulation in a modern urban society, there is a high possibility of living with more various stresses.

Of course, stress is a painful phenomenon. But on the other hand, it may be a good learning tool. Because people can look back on themselves through stress and even go a better way. If there is no stress to the people, who will look back and try to improve themselves, and what can we develop by whipping ourselves. If the saints were not stressed, what would they have been able to brush themselves up with? Stress is momentarily painful and difficult, but if you can find meaning and learning in the stress, it may be a good growth tool.

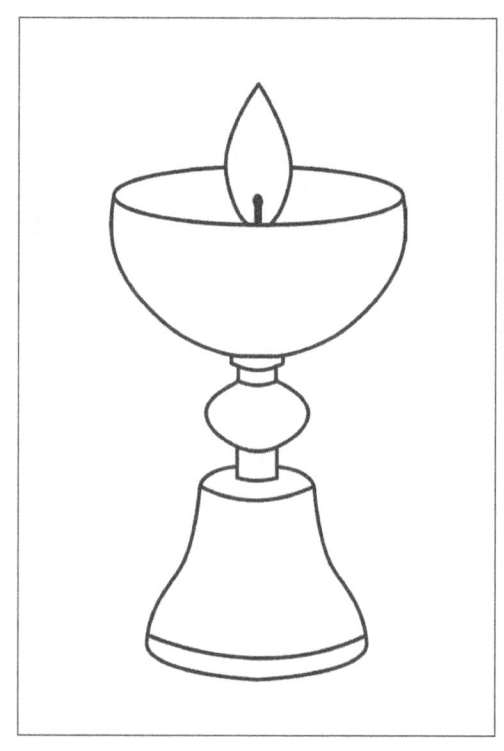

Butter lamp

You may wonder what you learn in stress. But if you makes it a turning point that stop and look back on what you have been doing through stress, you can take a look at the part you are currently facing and take it as an opportunity to move on.

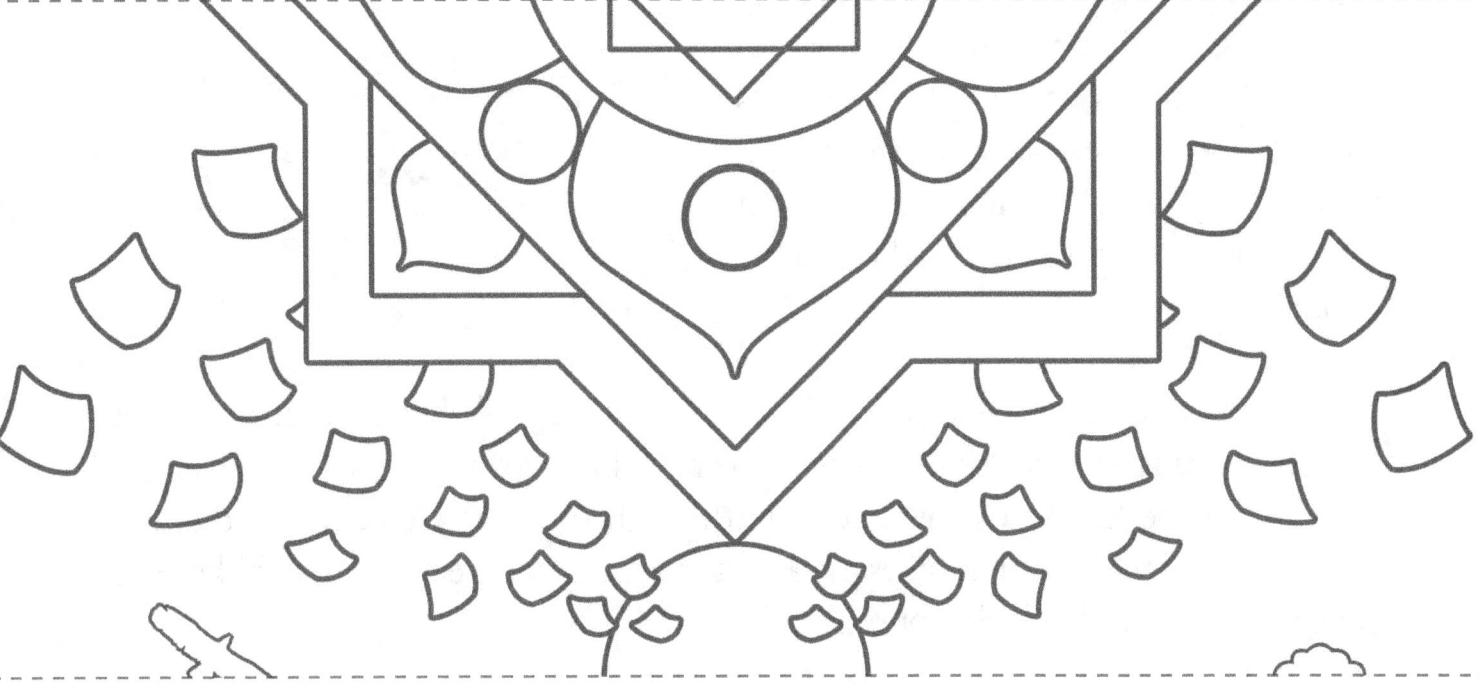

In the stress situation, a lot of minds are create. There may be some ways to relieve stress, but most of them are filled with thoughts to defend oneself, which causes the emotions to burn more and the judgment to dim over time. Under these circumstances, controlling emotions and lulling your thoughts are important priorities in relieving stress.

The coloring meditation process can be very effective in relieving the mind and stabilizing the mind by emitting the burning emotions. If you control your emotions and your thoughts diminish, you will be able to see the situation more objectively. Then you will have the opportunity to think about the meaning of the stress situation and what you need to learn through it. From there, stress becomes a turning point for learning. Then it evolves into a good opportunity to reflect on oneself rather than bitterness.

Modern people have a lot of thought. As the society became more complicated, the thoughts became more and more intense. In the sea of information, we live in so much information that we can not digest and in so many miscellaneous thoughts. In the vast amount of information and thoughts, you need to find out what you really need and learn. When you paint a design, most of your thoughts will slowly disappear. But things that you feel are really serious or important can still exist. And as coloring progresses, the thoughts are gathered into one, and then it is not an idle thought, is topic. In the course of coloring the design, unnecessary thoughts disappear and an important idea remains to be added to the depth.

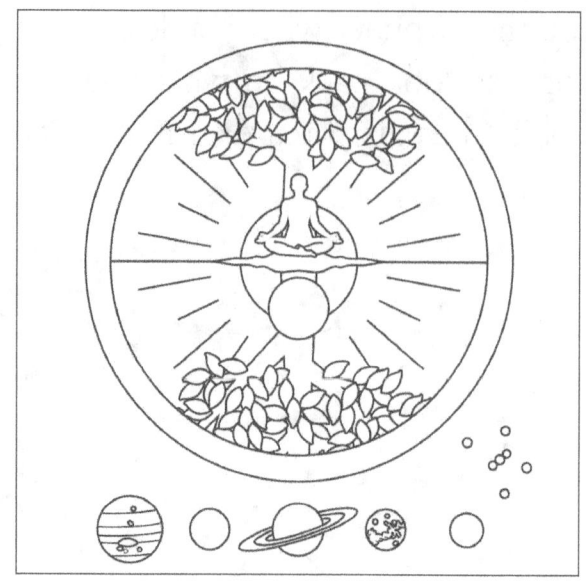

This is a process of self-reflection. These processes are probably the challenges that humans have to experience throughout their lifetime. For this reason, momentary stresses can be handled very effectively through only the Coloring-meditation processes, but the task that takes up a large part of each person's life will have to progress over a longer period of time.

We do not know where the end of the universe is. And hard to know where end of the self-reflection process for humans who exist as microcosm. However it is difficult for anyone to deny that it is the path that human beings should go.

One of the hallmarks of Coloring-meditation is that no advance preparation is required. It will be rare and easy to approach for stress relief and self-reflection. Just painting the design, reduces the stress and goes to the same state as meditation. Coloring meditation is also very easy. All you need is a colored pencil (or other coloring tool). Then you can have time to look back at yourself. And there is no rule there. The design is made up of lines, but it is just a line. It is not a bounded border. It is just a representation of the universe. The universe exists both inside and outside the line. Therefore, there is no restriction or rule for you to color the design. You can either ignore the line or paint on it, leave it empty, or fill it. The best way is to just paint what you want from your body as you like.

If the mandala is something abstract and intangible, then the mountains and backgrounds of Himalayas will be a link to concrete and tangible phenomena. By arranging the abstract and the concrete, we are able to approach it more fully and deeply.

What is mandala ?

Mandala is a guide to enlightenment to unite with the essence of the universe.

Mandala is the Sanskrit word for "essence(Manda)" and "possessive(la)". That is the picture and guide map which contains the essence of the universe, it means "circle".

The symmetrical composition based on circles, which is a characteristic form of mandala designs, has been shown and used mostly in Buddhist cultures such as India, Tibet and Nepal. If you look at the lotus pattern which is a typical Asia pattern, there are symmetry forms based on circles. This form can be seen as an old symbol of mankind, and it can be seen as one of the unconscious forms that humans want to unite with divinity.

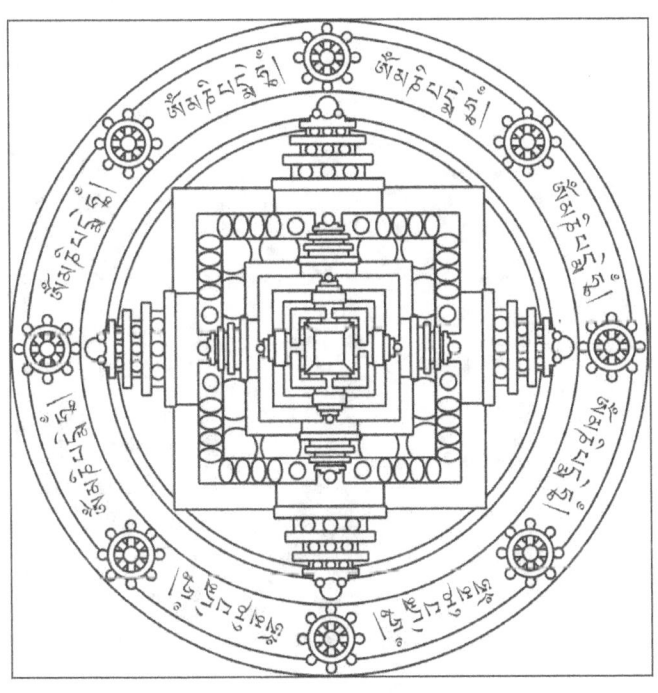

Mandala is usually based on circles and rectangles. It is a two-dimensional figure, but it is a complex representation of multidimensional time and space.

In modern times, Mandala was known as a means of psychotherapy and self-reflection by psychologist Carl Gustav Jung. Currently, mandala designs are used in a variety of ways from psychotherapy to cultivation of children's concentration and creativity, and as a way of self-reflection of adults.

Benefits and effects of Coloring-meditation

The biggest advantage of coloring meditation is that it can relieve stress and bring stability to mind and body through inner communication.

People are exposed to a variety of psychological stress situations from time to time, and when you do Coloring-meditation, you can relieve your stress and calm your mind and expect a variety of other effects.

As your mind stabilizes, your concentration and creativity will naturally increase, and you will be able to find clues to your own problems and concerns. You usually spend a lot of time and effort to get these things, but you can draw them yourself in a relatively short amount of time through the Coloring-meditation process.

Here are some of the main effects expected from the Coloring-meditation process.

1. Body-mind harmony

By recognizing and understanding the current situation in a stable state of mind, it helps the body and mind to harmonize and move in the right direction.

2. Improve concentration

Through Coloring meditation, you naturally acquire the process of disappearing your distracting thoughts, helping you to improve your concentration.

3. Improve creativity and ideas

Creativity is the ability to express your own unique creativity in yourself, so you can help yourself to develop your own unique creativity through understanding and knowing yourself.

4. Stress relief

Stress is a kind of energy stagnation phenomenon, by unravelling and releasing your own blocked energy, the stress naturally decreases through Coloring meditation.

5. Energy charging

By looking at yourself through Coloring meditation, you turn the energy from outside to inside and naturally fill the energy and create vitality.

6. Increased problem solving ability

By reducing the number of unnecessary thoughts that prevent you from seeing the problem right away, it helps you to identify key issues and look at the situation in an objective way to find solutions.

7. Self-exploration and reflection

Through Coloring meditation, you have time to explore on yourself, healing your lives to live more rewarding and enriching lives.

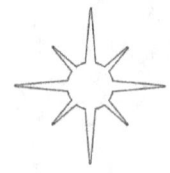

How to Coloring meditation

It is the best way to do what you want to do as your mind goes.
Please apply according to your situation or mood by referring to the
following method.

1. Create a tranquil environment

It is best to create a quiet, unobstructed environment.
Depending on your taste, you can create quiet surroundings with classical or
meditative music or your favorite music, lighting, aroma, incense and more.

2. Select the design

Choose a coloring design according to the feeling of the day. Or you can
paint the coloring design in the order of books. Look at the selected design
and draw (feel) how to paint for a while.

3. Painting designs

Regardless of the line, color it freely to the heart.
You can use various coloring tools such as colored pencils, crayons, pen,
marker, and pastel to suit your taste. Among them, colored pencils are the
most used because they are easy to use and easy to color.

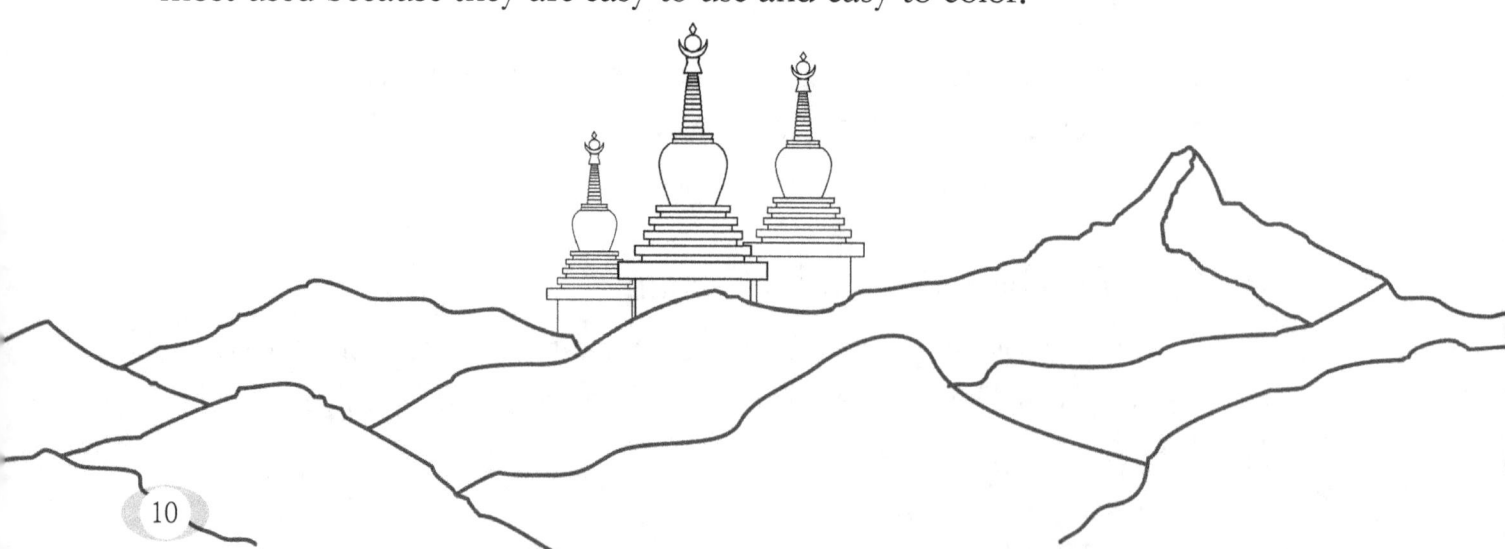

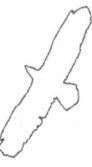

4. Writing what comes to mind

After coloring is over, write your own title and write down your feelings, thinkings, or other things that come to mind in the space provided in the book.

If you do not have to write anything, just put the pen on the book and write down on it. If you write down your thoughts a little bit, the writing will be continued. Even if you try to write without thinking, it is like writing from your own inside. If you read it again after writing it, it will be a good reference material to understand the current situation.

Sometimes, when you write, you find that key to solving the problem or you have something to learn in a completely different place than you think. This process of coloring and writing will help you to understand the current situation.

Sometimes when you are under a lot of stress, or when your head is so complicated that you have a lot of things to clean up, you may feel that a single Coloring meditation process is not enough. In such a case, it is best to take 2-3 consecutive Coloring meditation sessions to loosen the accumulated or entangled things. After coloring a design, write down the things that come to mind, and immediately follow it to color and write the following design.

If you are under strong stress, you will get explosive energy from the inside, so you will have less time and easier to coloring. Also, when you organize it as a writing, there are many things to solve, so many articles can come out.

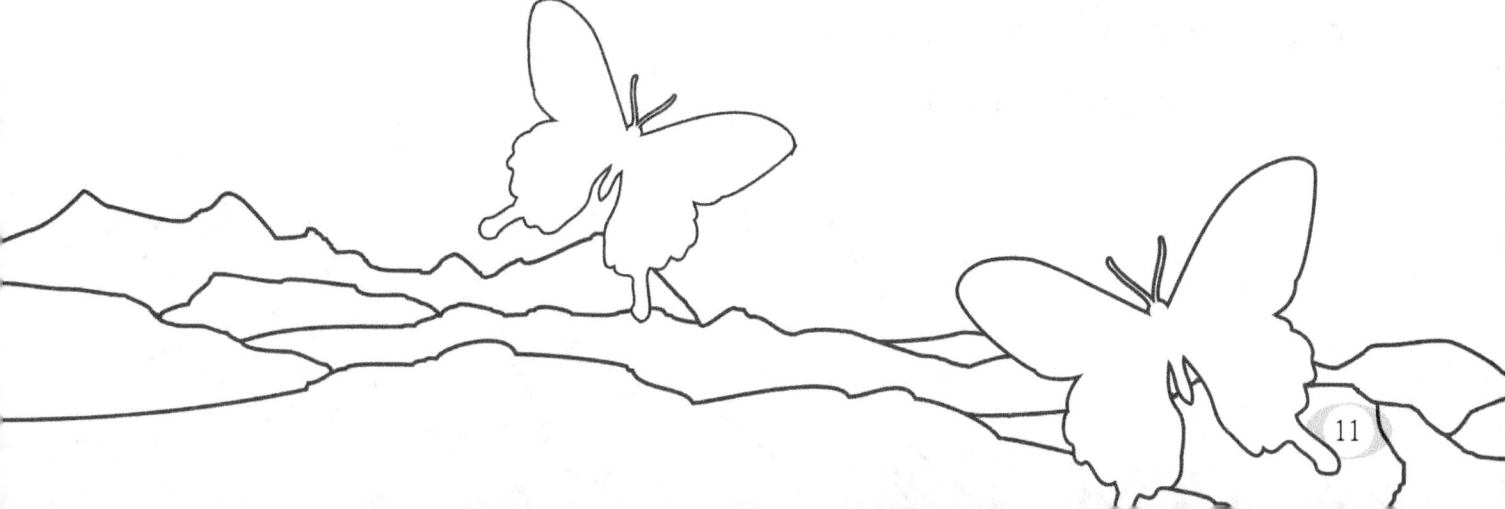

Deep look inside at the question

It is a meditation process for those who want a deeper experience after the coloring and writing process, or who still have questions and want to look into the question more deeply.

I. Posture

The posture will be in any posture to straighten the waist. Burmese (simple cross-legged) position is comfortable. The lotus position and half lotus position (sitting with one's legs half-crossed, as in lotus position) is good. Or a sitting position on a chair is also good. Sit straight and relax your shoulders in any position.

1. Straighten your waist.
2. In that state, relax your shoulder and body .
3. Put your arms down naturally on your thighs.
4. Close your mouth and have your tongue gently attach the palate.
5. You can close your eyes, and it's good to lay down your eyes and lightly open.
6. And relax in your nose and relax your breath a few times until the breath is stable.

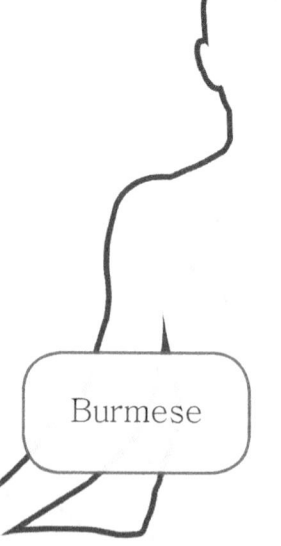

Burmese

II. Look into the question

If you have a question that comes to mind in the process of Coloring meditation, after asking questions about it, and look carefully at what comes to my mind.

If rise more important and meaningful questions in the process of observing your mind, look into it.

You will find a better solution than usual because your mind is more calm and witty than ever before through Coloring meditation process.

There is a possibility that the solution will not be seen immediately. However, through this process, you will have a deeper understanding of the problem and a more positive and broader perspective..

※ If you do not have any questions, please refer to the example below.

* What do I learn here?
* What do I really want now?
* What do I need most now?
* What is the most important thing for me right now?

※ There is also a way to ask questions about the title you wrote after you painted.

* What does [my title] mean to me now?

It is a natural phenomenon of the mind that various thoughts arise. When that happens, do not fret over whatever it is, and take a closer look at it. The thoughts will immediately change color or disappear according to its importance. When you look closely, your distracting thoughts lose their power. On the other hand, meaningful thoughts add depth.

It is enough that short time to start, and increase it gradually. Good for 5 minutes, good for 1 minute. A short time of just one minute will be a meaningful time.

Himalayan scenery

Himalayas

Himalaya range derives from the Sanskrit that mean "Abode of Snow". It is a mountain range with 14 peaks of over 8000m including the highest Everest (Everest 8,848m), K2 (8,611m) and Annapurna (8,091m). It is located in Pakistan, India, China (Tibet), Bhutan and Nepal. It is also the origin of the Indus, Ganges, Brahmaputra and Yangtze. The roof of the world or the land of the soul and called "the Mother Goddess of the World(Chomolungma)" in Tibet. The Himalayas are now the center of the earth's spiritual culture, giving the world a lot of spiritual inspiration and home of the mandala. Aad it is also a place of undergo spiritual training of high priest of Buddhism and seeker of truth.

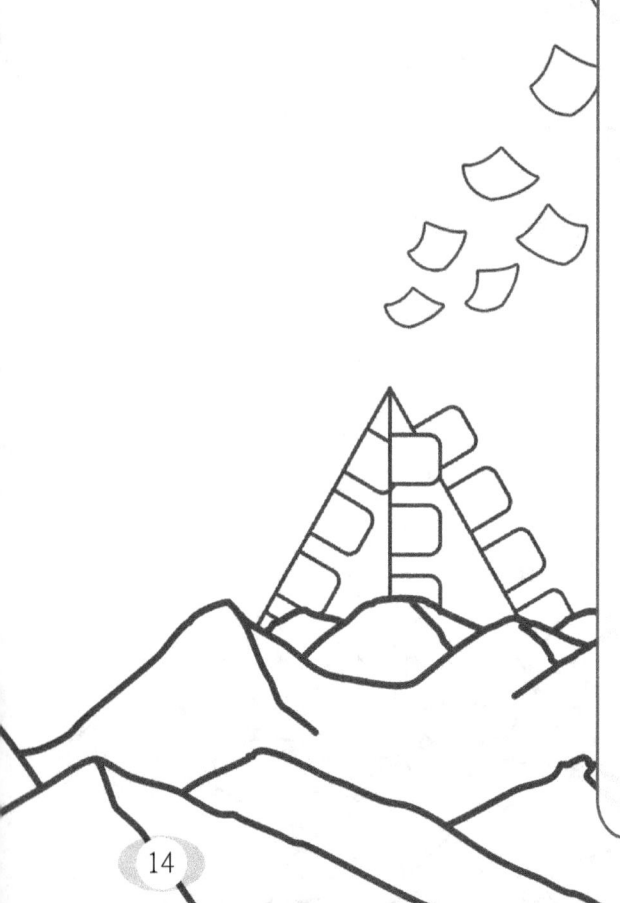

Tharchog, Lungda

With its colorful prayer flags on long lines, you can easily see Tibet wherever you are, such as temples, village entrances, hills, family houses, bridge trees, tombs, tree trees and big rocks.

"Tharchog" and "Lungda" are used in combination. Tharchog is mainly printed with scriptures, and Lungda has horse drawings. In Tibetan, 'Lung' means wind and 'da' means horse. It means "horse of the wind." It has a meaning that wants to communicate quickly with God through horse like wind. These were originally used to mark milestones or sacred places, but gradually they have been turned into uses for personal wishes and well-being. Things made of paper climb high and scatter them in the sky.

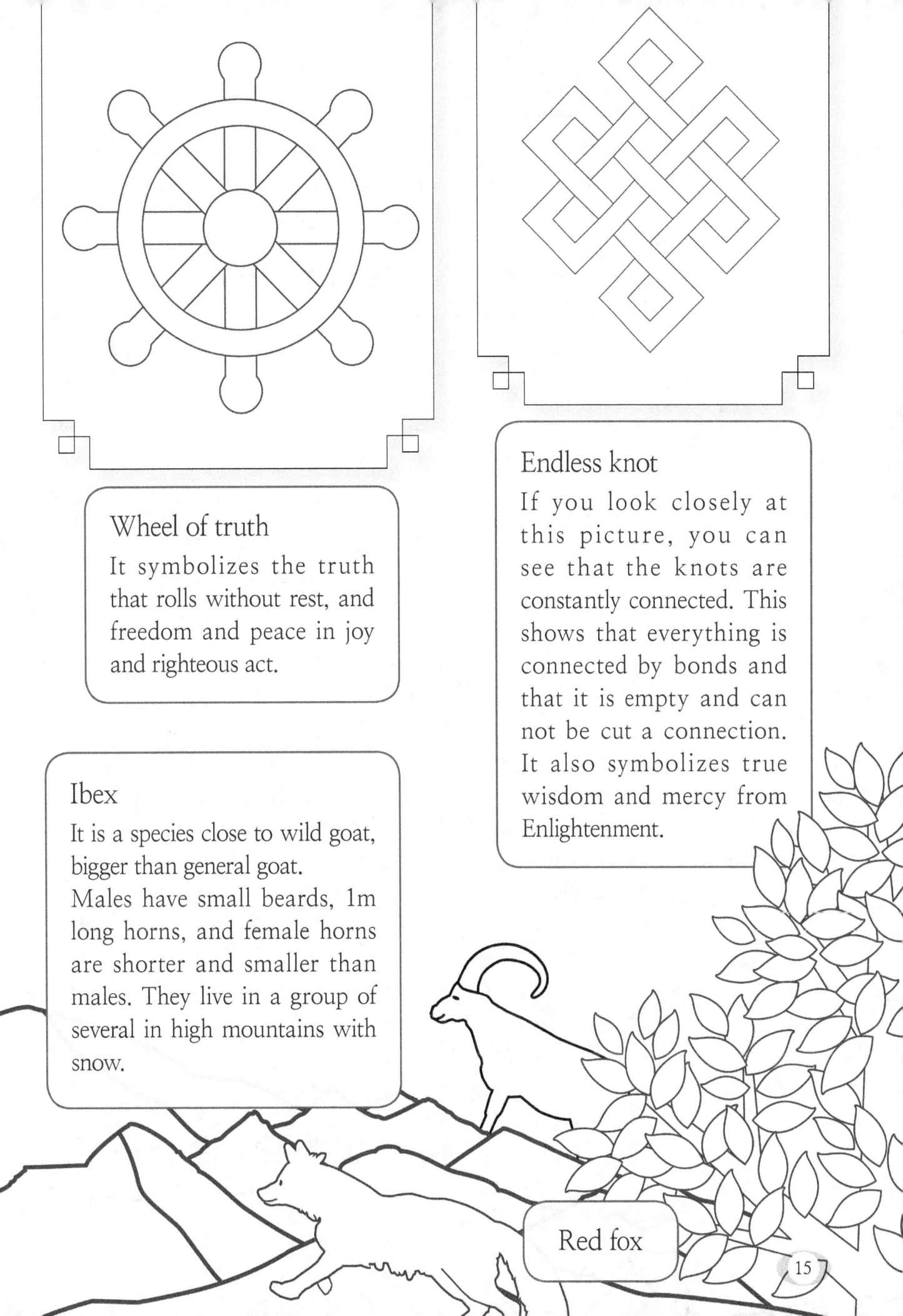

Wheel of truth

It symbolizes the truth that rolls without rest, and freedom and peace in joy and righteous act.

Endless knot

If you look closely at this picture, you can see that the knots are constantly connected. This shows that everything is connected by bonds and that it is empty and can not be cut a connection. It also symbolizes true wisdom and mercy from Enlightenment.

Ibex

It is a species close to wild goat, bigger than general goat.
Males have small beards, 1m long horns, and female horns are shorter and smaller than males. They live in a group of several in high mountains with snow.

Red fox

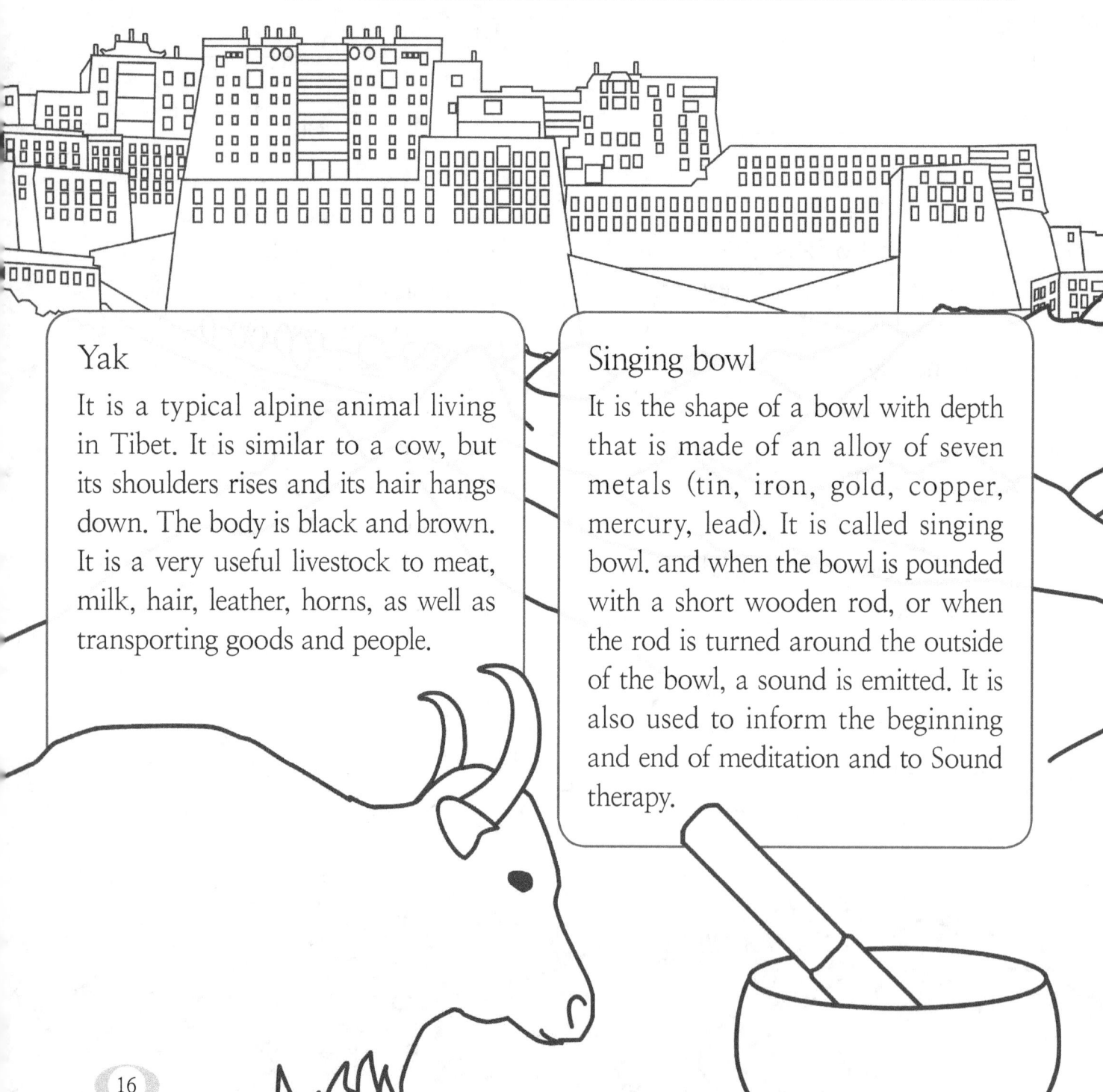

Potala palace

It is a palace in Lhasa, Tibet Autonomous Region of China. It was the residence of the Dalai Lama and the headquarters of Tibetan Buddhism. It was registered as a UNESCO World Heritage Site in 1994.

The length of the Potala palace is 360m, north and south is 270m, and the height is 13 stories high and reaches 117m.

Yak

It is a typical alpine animal living in Tibet. It is similar to a cow, but its shoulders rises and its hair hangs down. The body is black and brown. It is a very useful livestock to meat, milk, hair, leather, horns, as well as transporting goods and people.

Singing bowl

It is the shape of a bowl with depth that is made of an alloy of seven metals (tin, iron, gold, copper, mercury, lead). It is called singing bowl. and when the bowl is pounded with a short wooden rod, or when the rod is turned around the outside of the bowl, a sound is emitted. It is also used to inform the beginning and end of meditation and to Sound therapy.

Snow leopard

It is the highest carnivorous animal of the Himalayan alpine region, similar to a leopard, but smaller in size and has a long, thick tail. The body is pale yellowish brown and grayish white and has dark brown or black dot patterns.

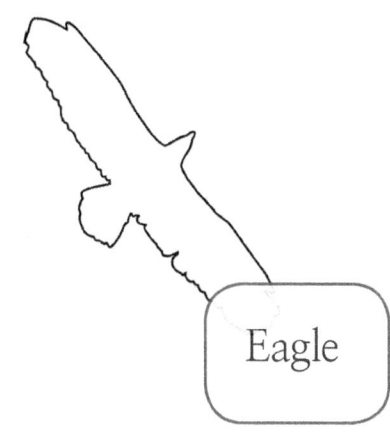

Eagle

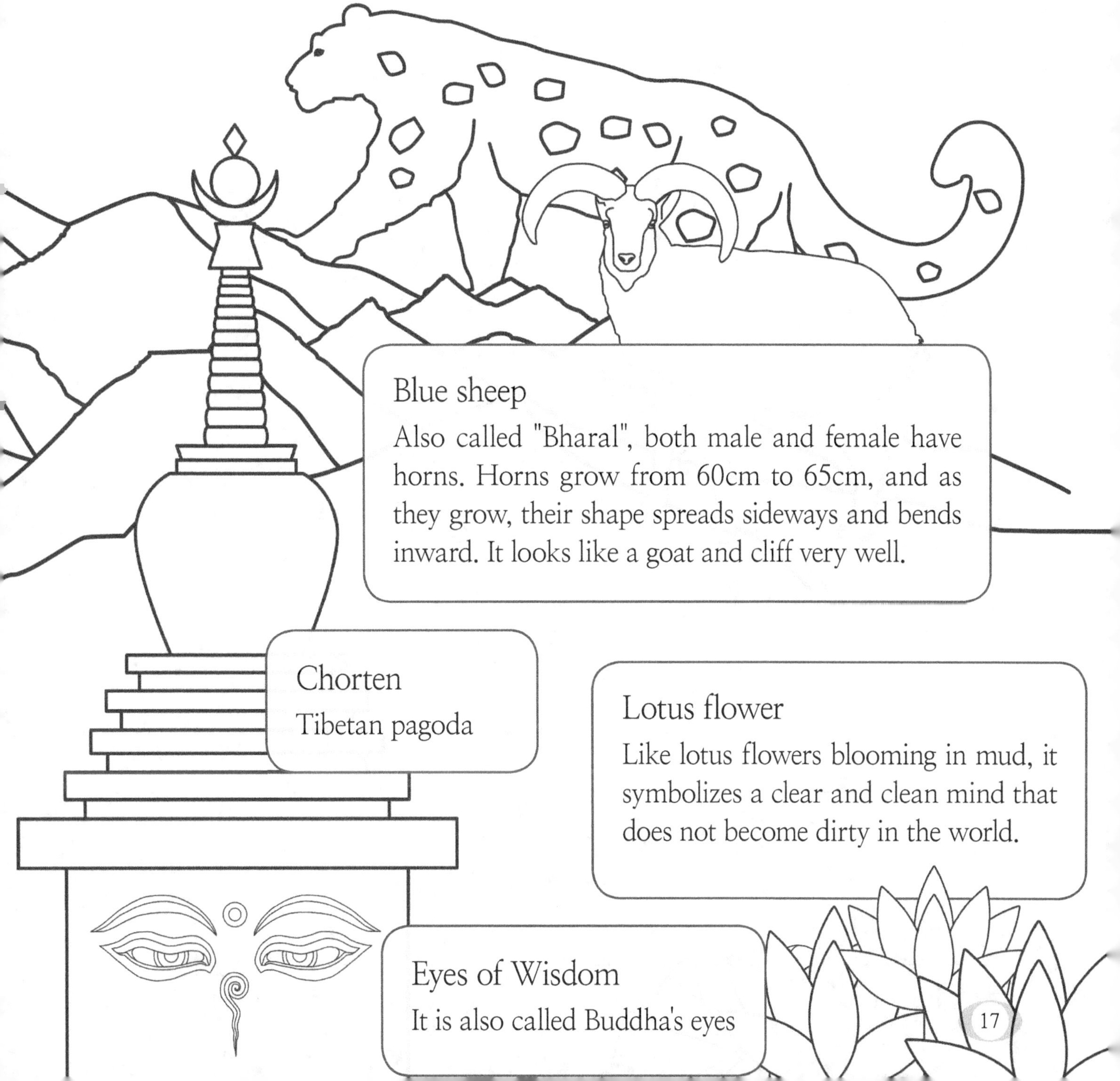

Blue sheep

Also called "Bharal", both male and female have horns. Horns grow from 60cm to 65cm, and as they grow, their shape spreads sideways and bends inward. It looks like a goat and cliff very well.

Chorten

Tibetan pagoda

Lotus flower

Like lotus flowers blooming in mud, it symbolizes a clear and clean mind that does not become dirty in the world.

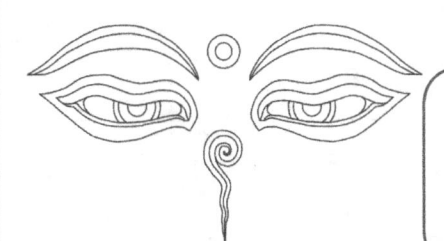

Eyes of Wisdom

It is also called Buddha's eyes

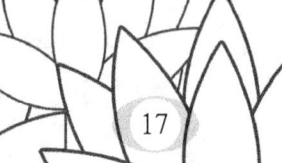

Title :

Now what comes to mind, feelings, thoughts

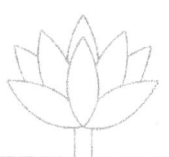

In short

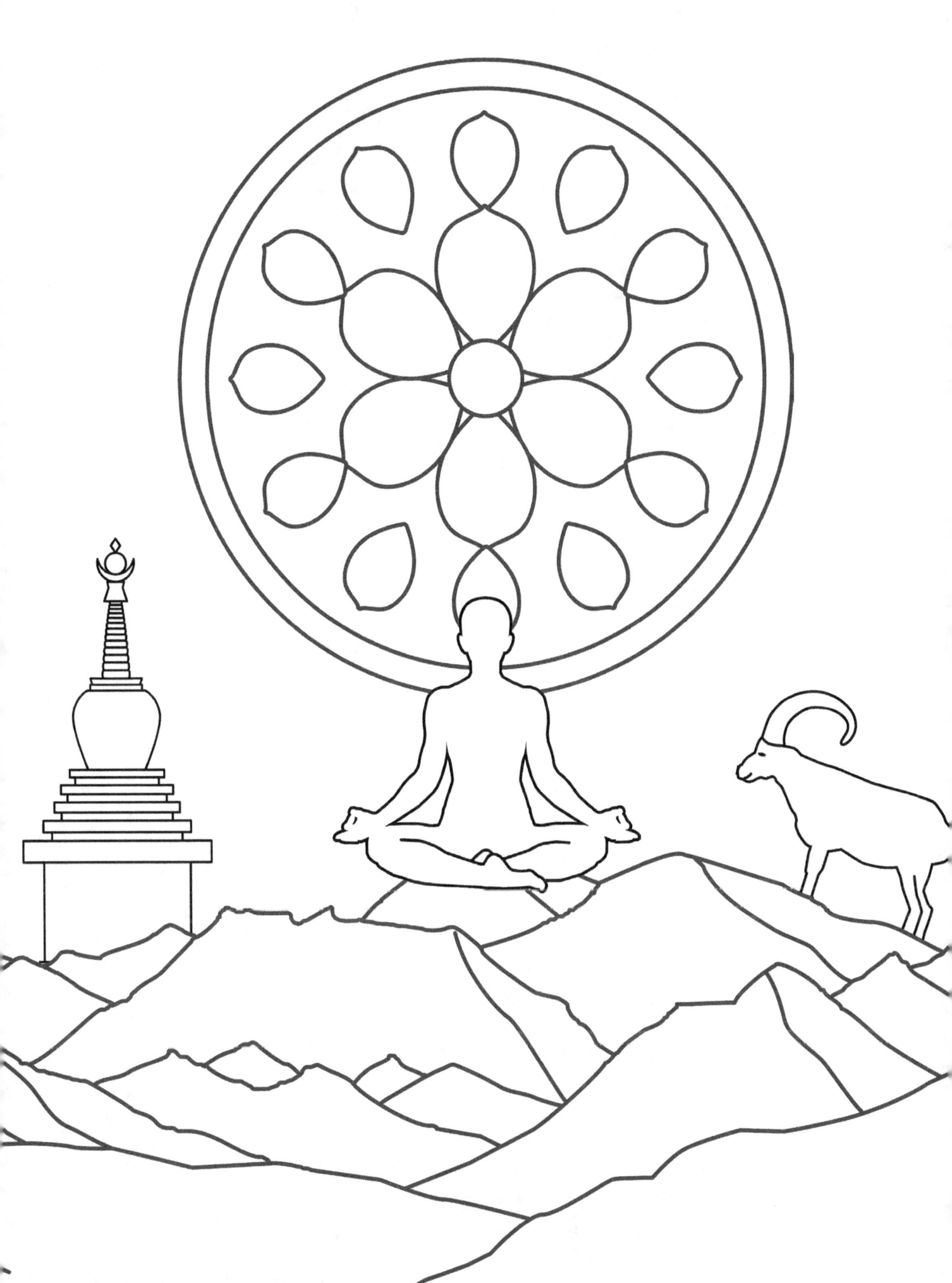

Title :

Now what comes to mind, feelings, thoughts

In short

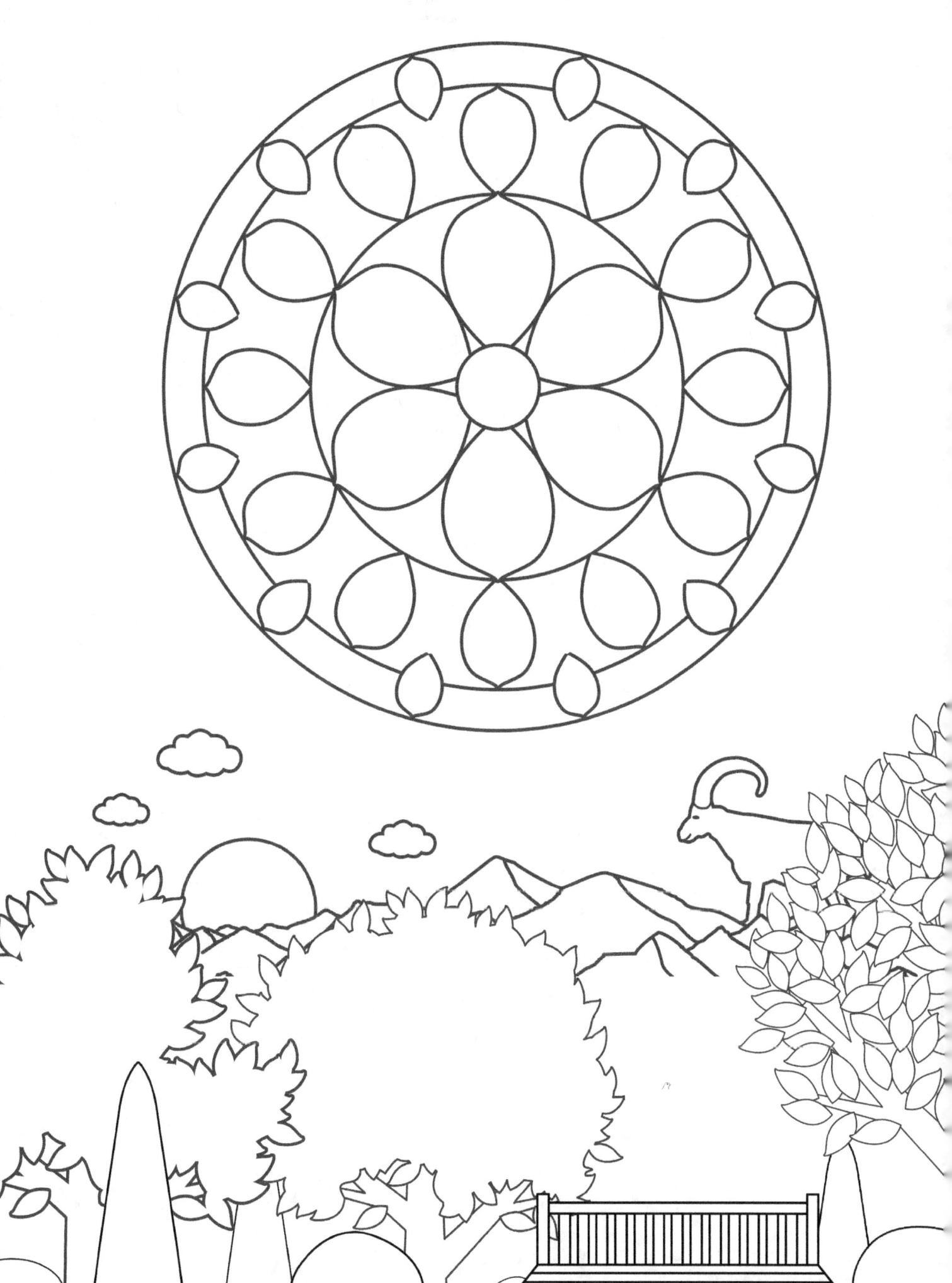

Title :

Now what comes to mind, feelings, thoughts

In short

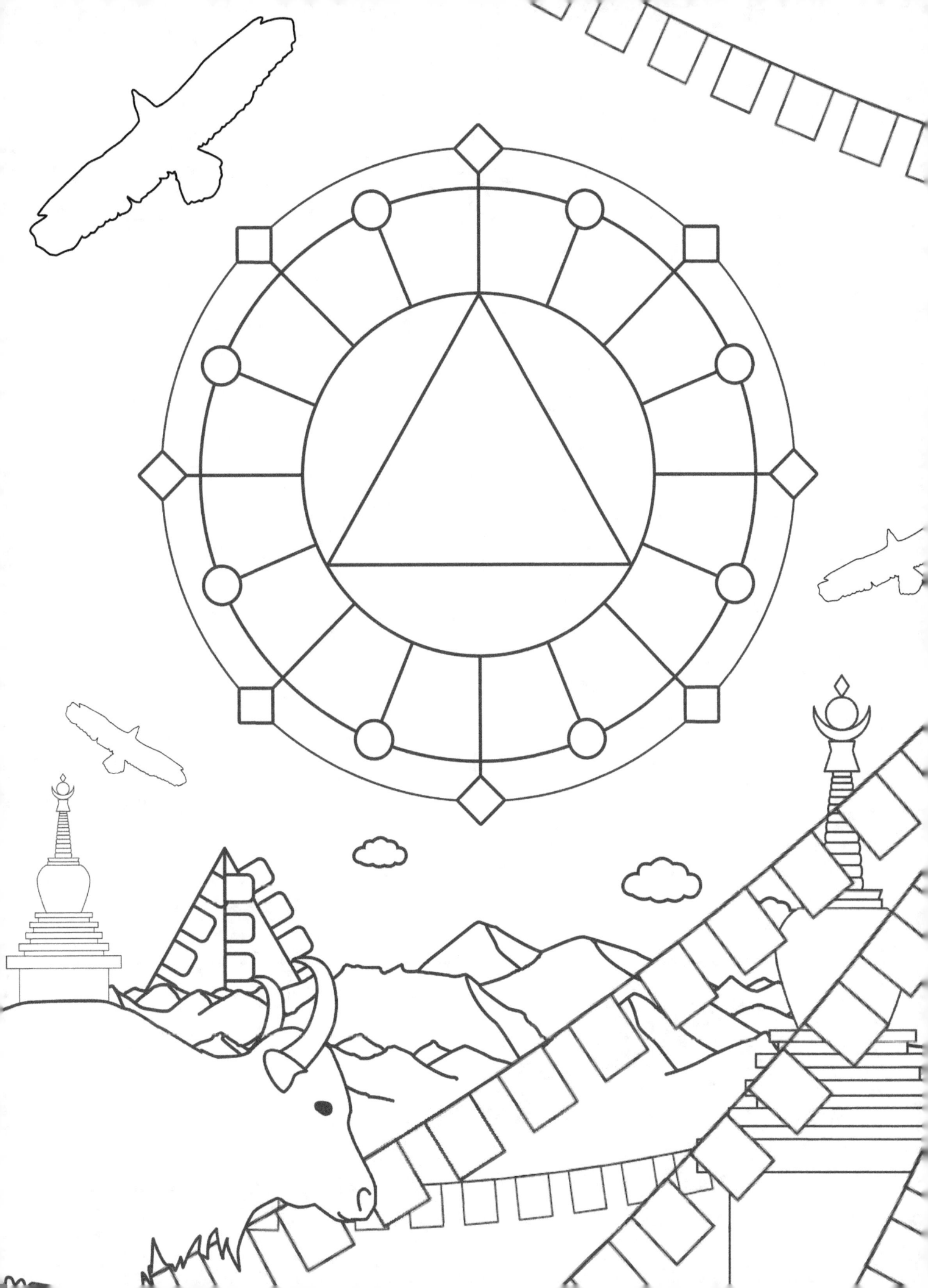

Title :

Now what comes to mind, feelings, thoughts

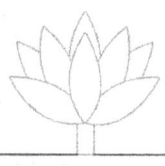

In short

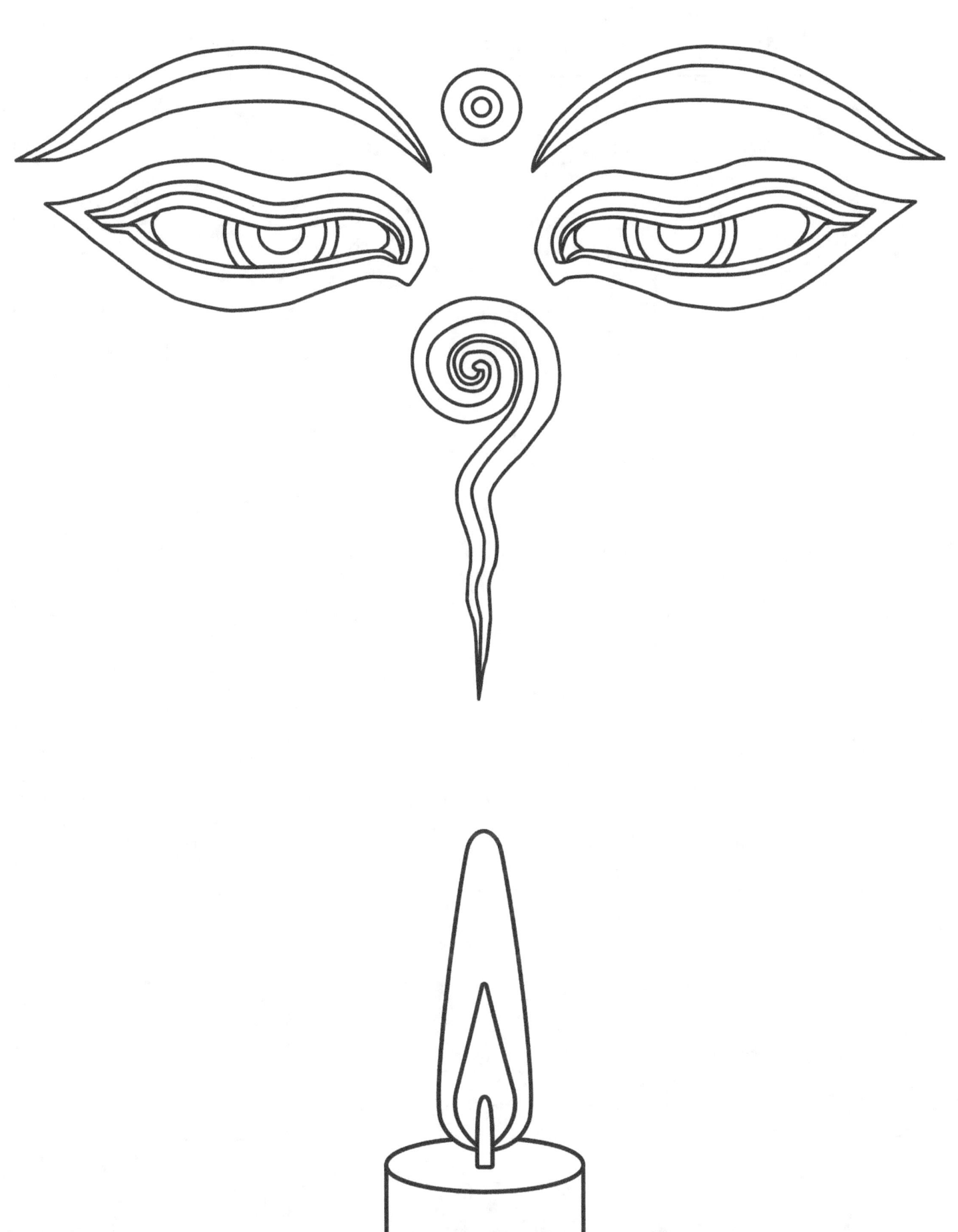

Title :

Now what comes to mind, feelings, thoughts

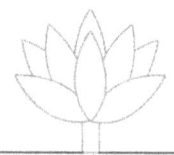

In short

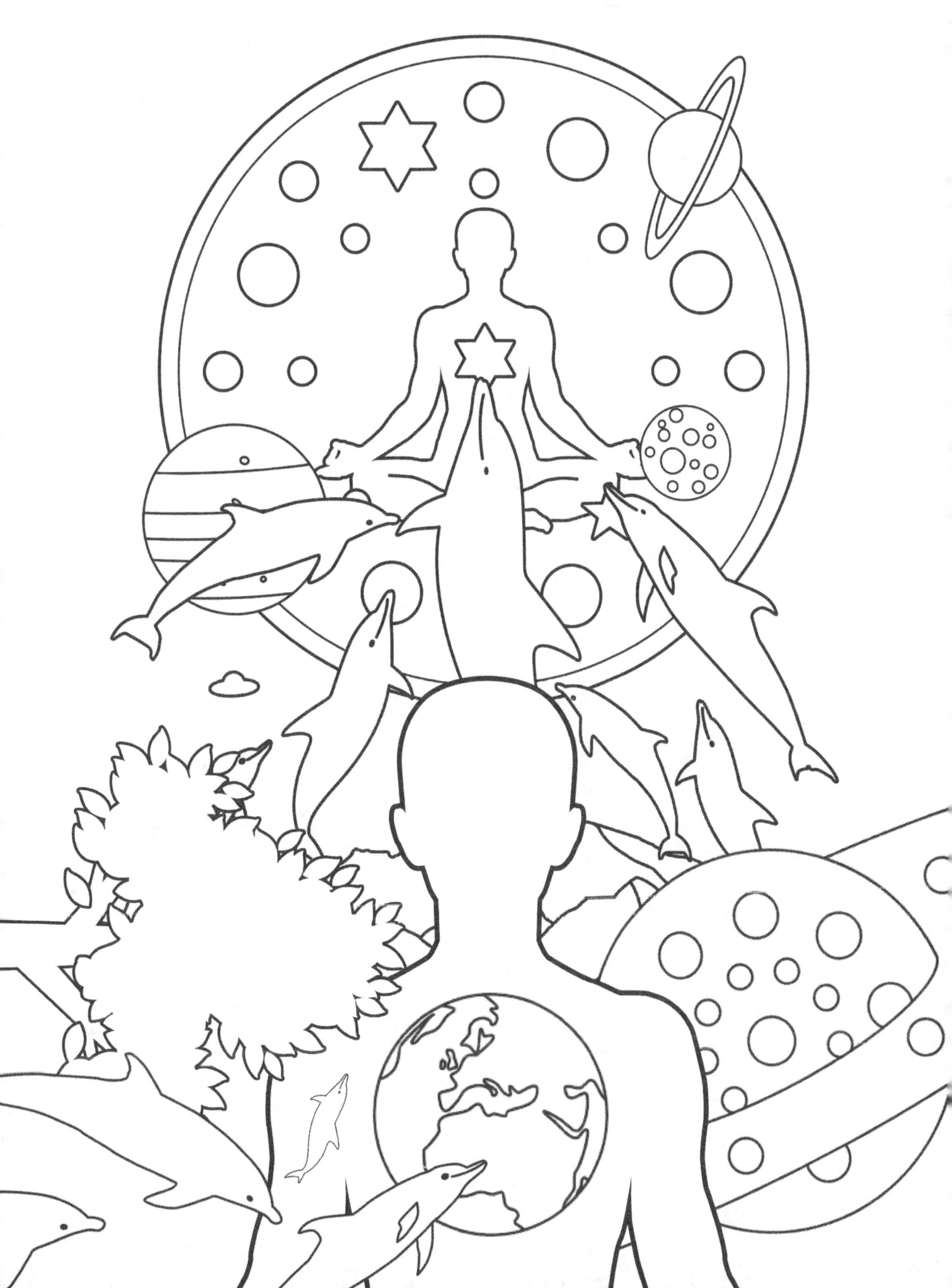

Title :

Now what comes to mind, feelings, thoughts

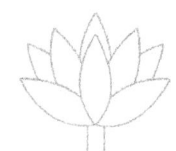

In short

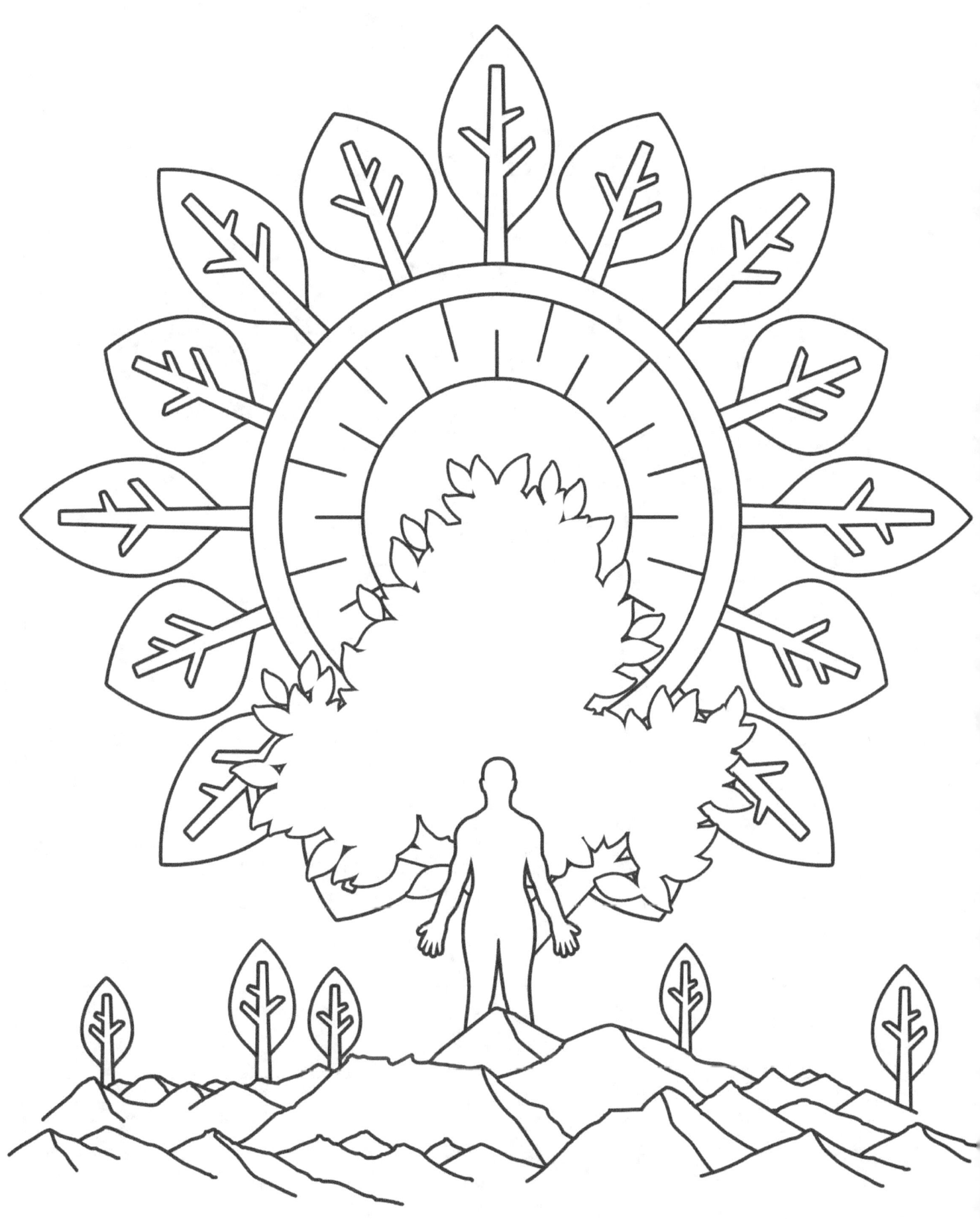

Title :

Now what comes to mind, feelings, thoughts

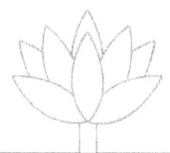

In short

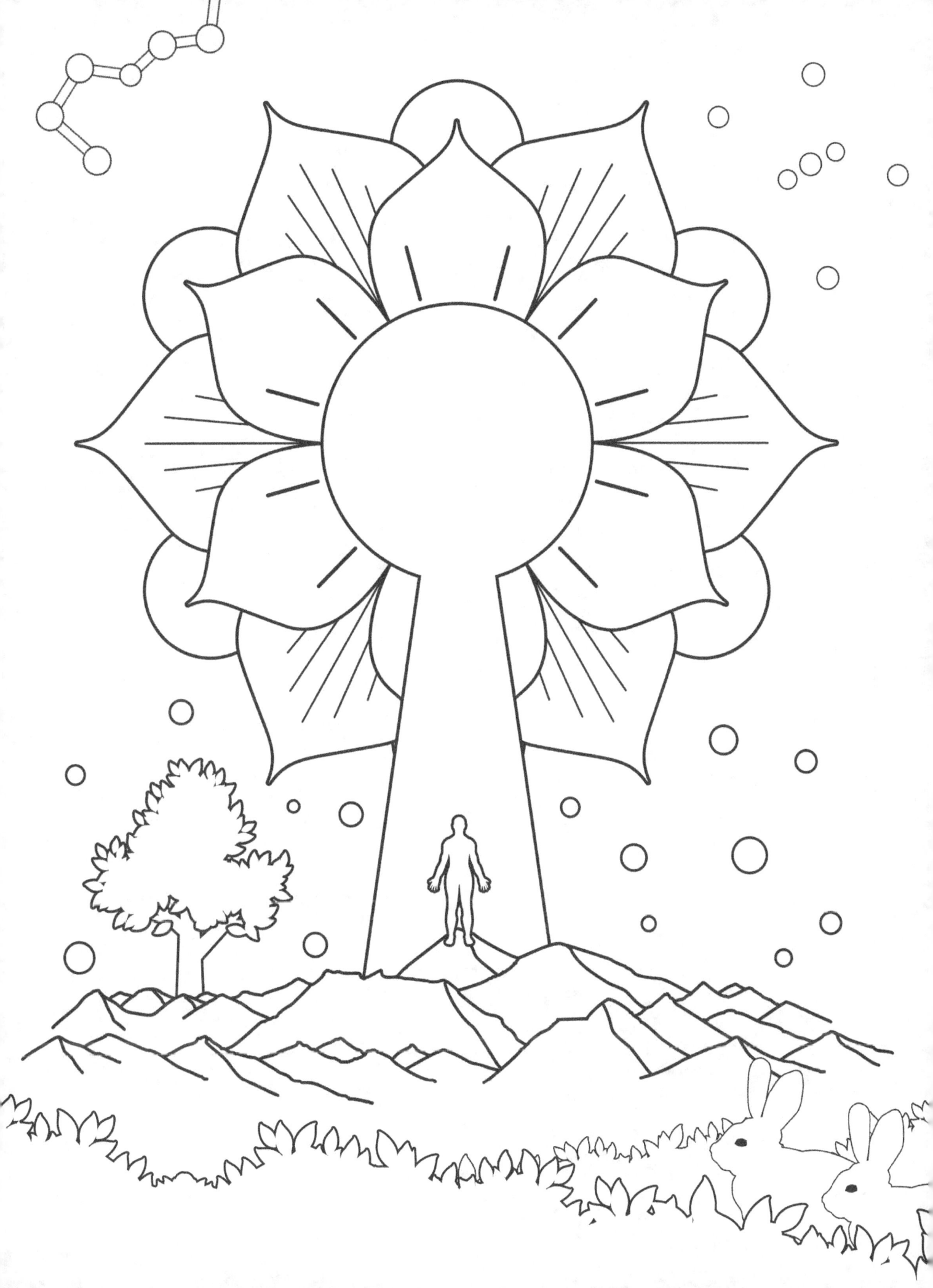

Title :

Now what comes to mind, feelings, thoughts

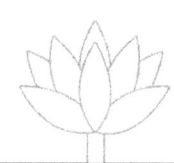

In short

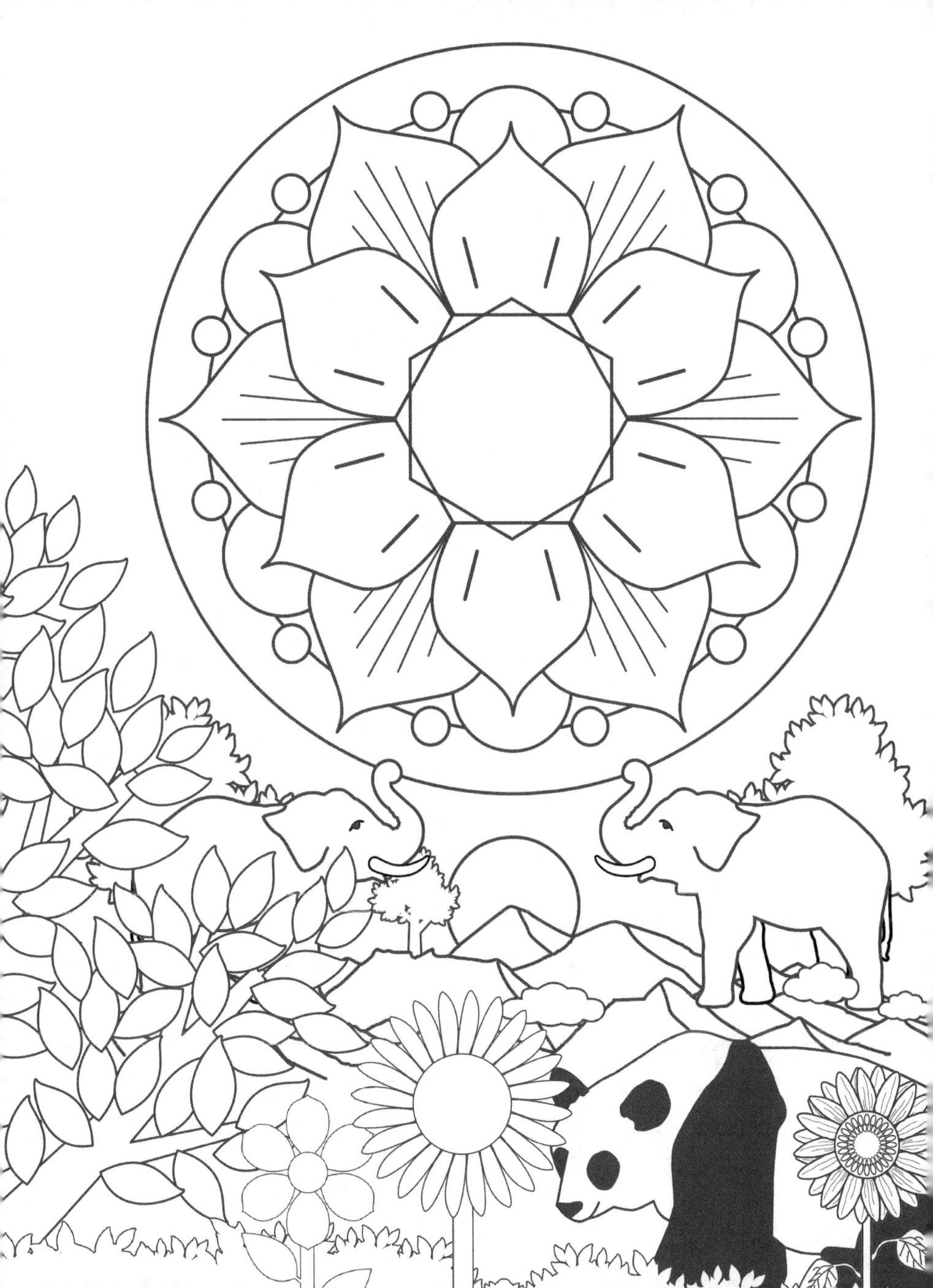

Title :

Now what comes to mind, feelings, thoughts

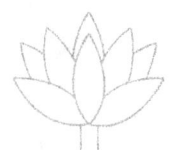

In short

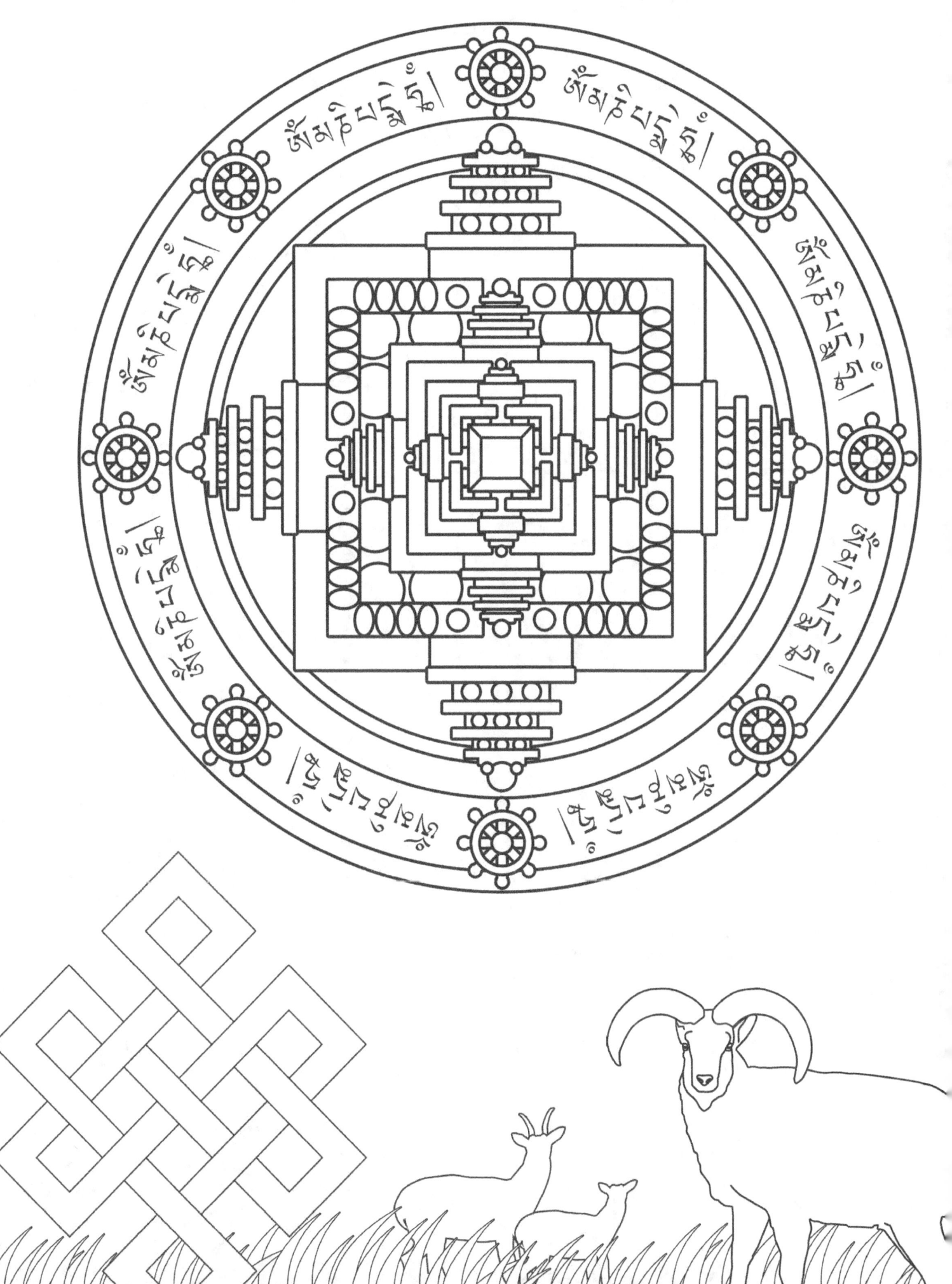

Title :

Now what comes to mind, feelings, thoughts

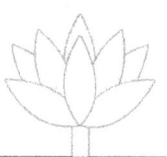

In short

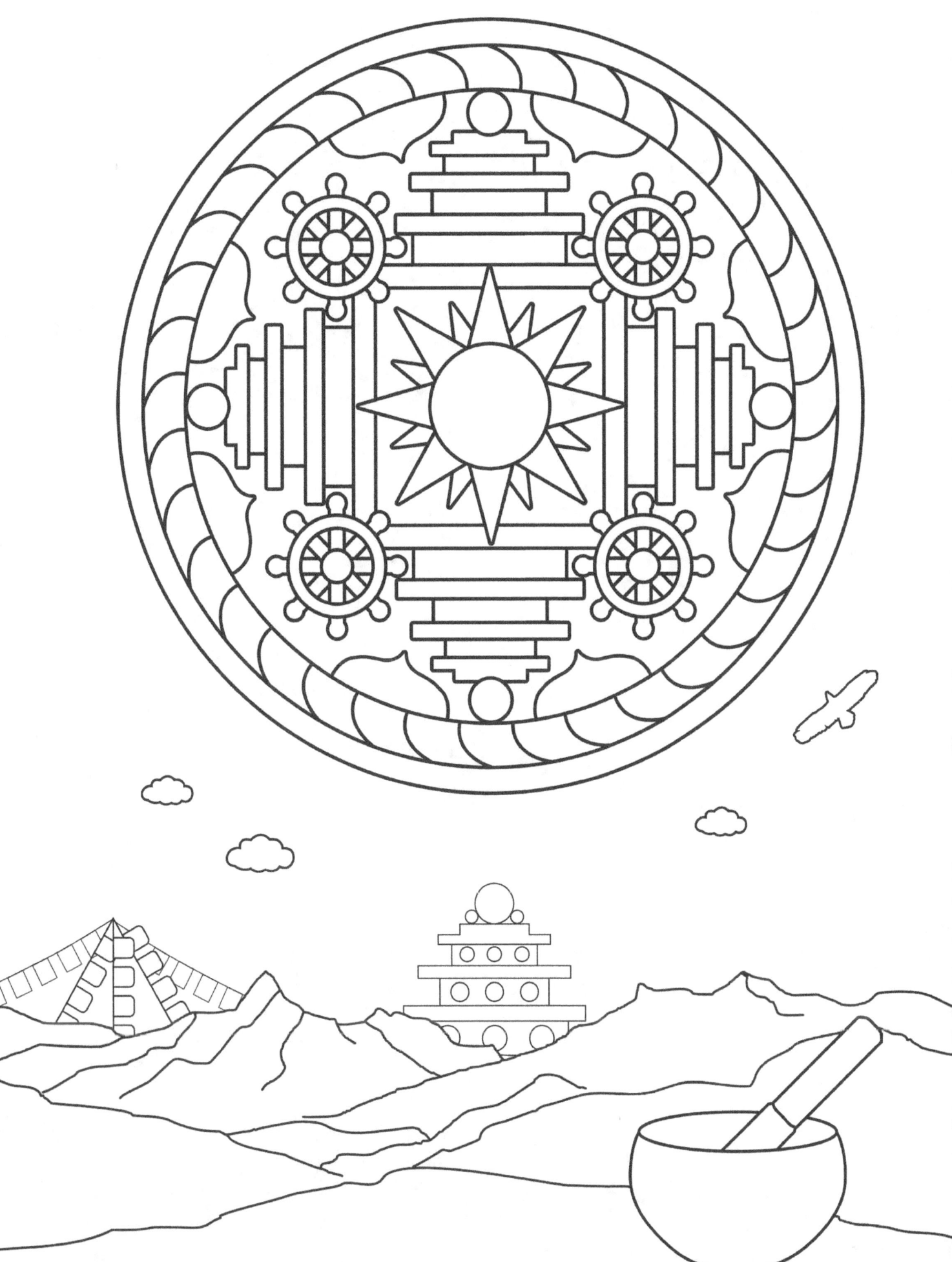

Title :

Now what comes to mind, feelings, thoughts

In short

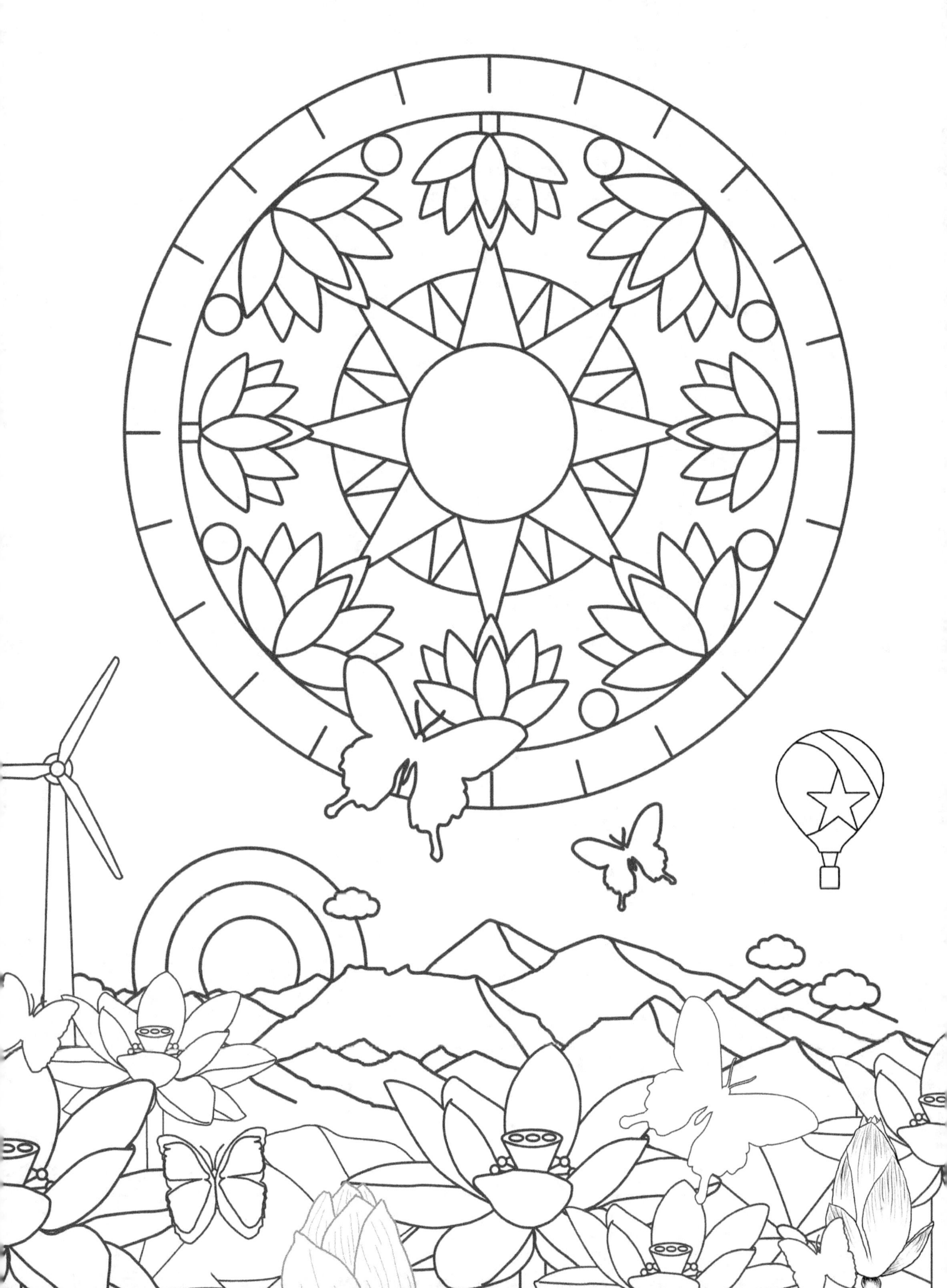

Title :

Now what comes to mind, feelings, thoughts

In short

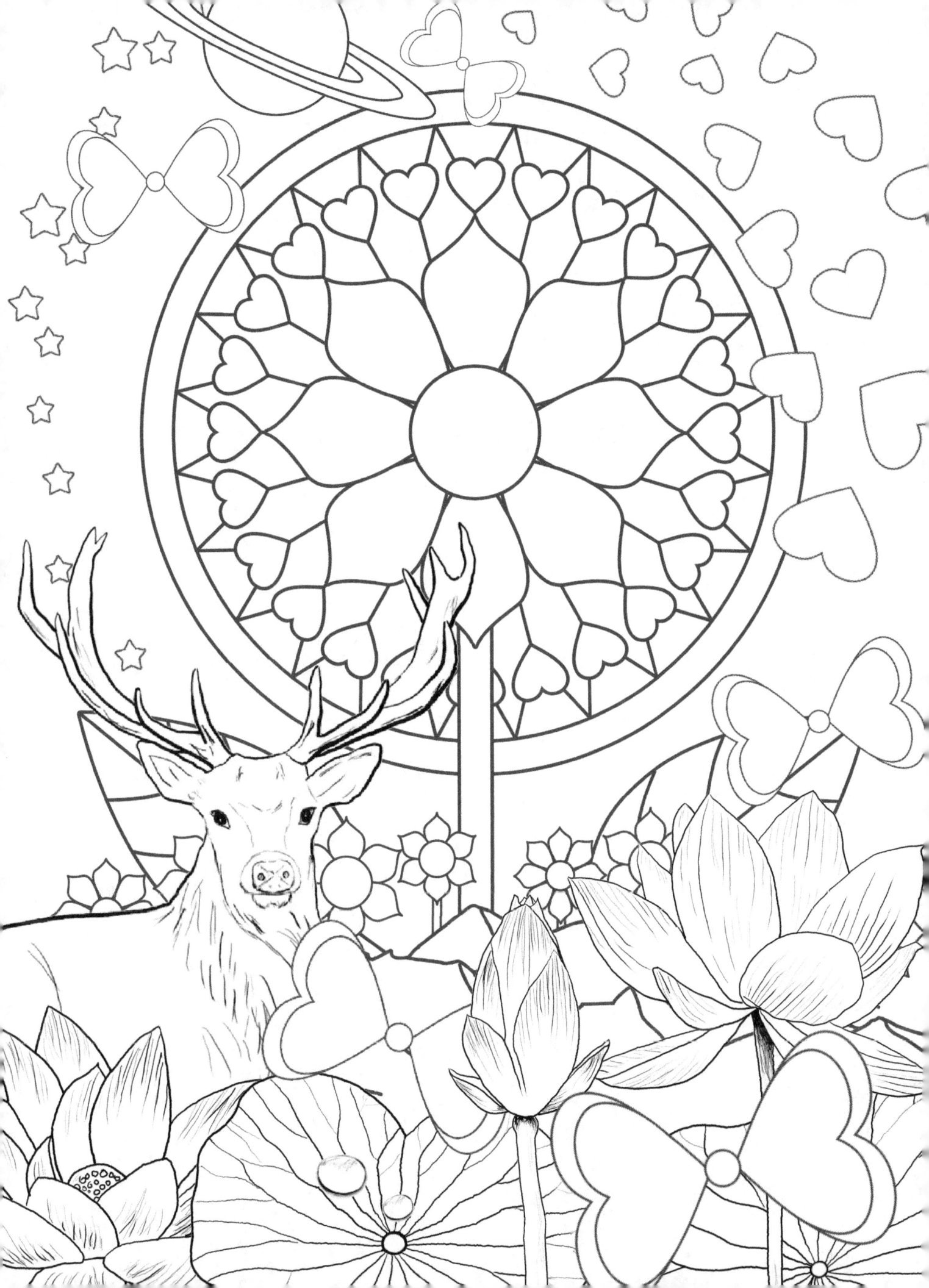

Title :

Now what comes to mind, feelings, thoughts

In short

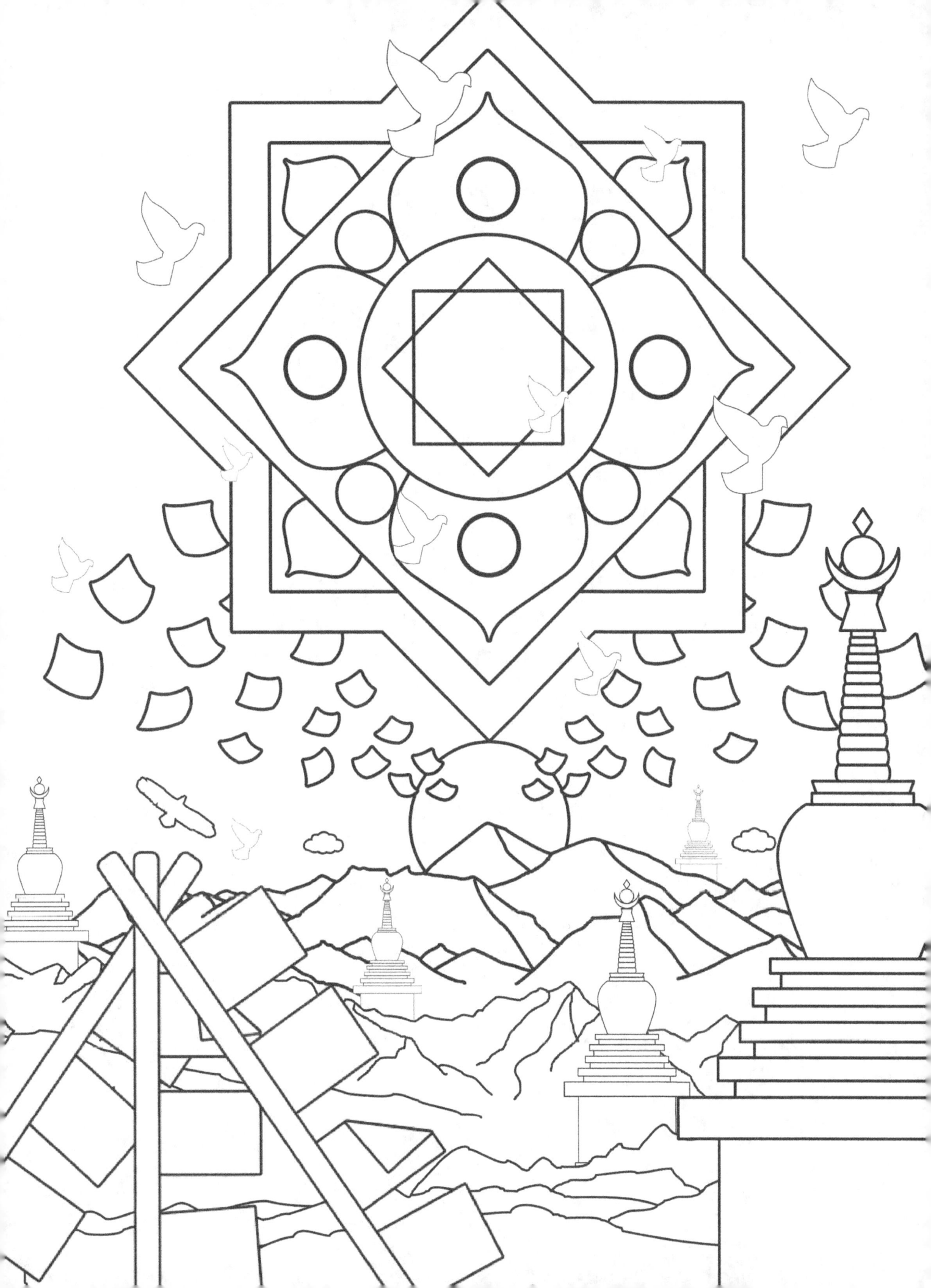

Title :

Now what comes to mind, feelings, thoughts

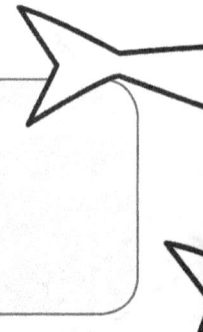

In short

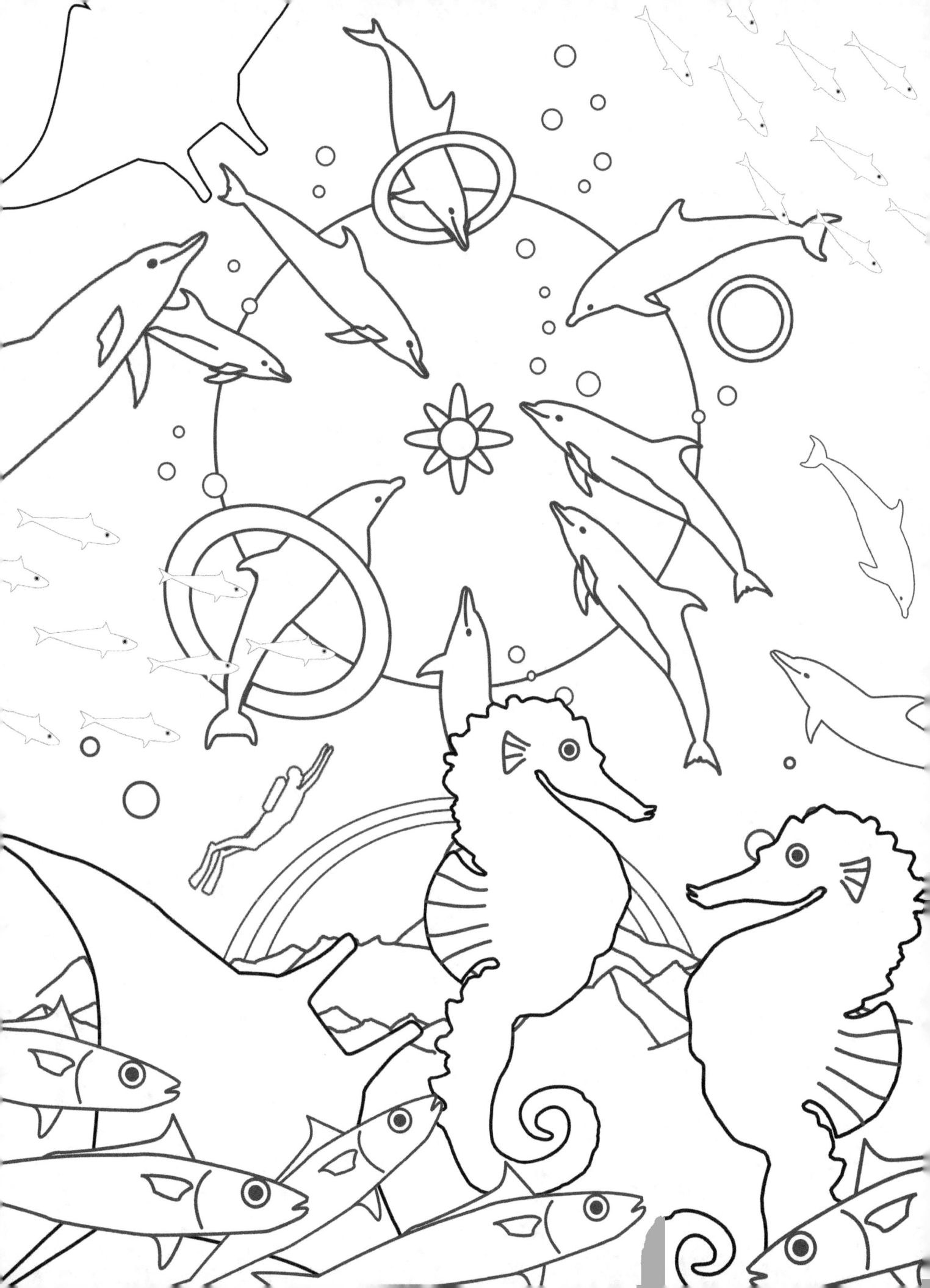

Title :

Now what comes to mind, feelings, thoughts

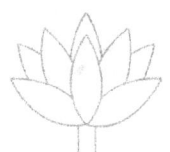

In short

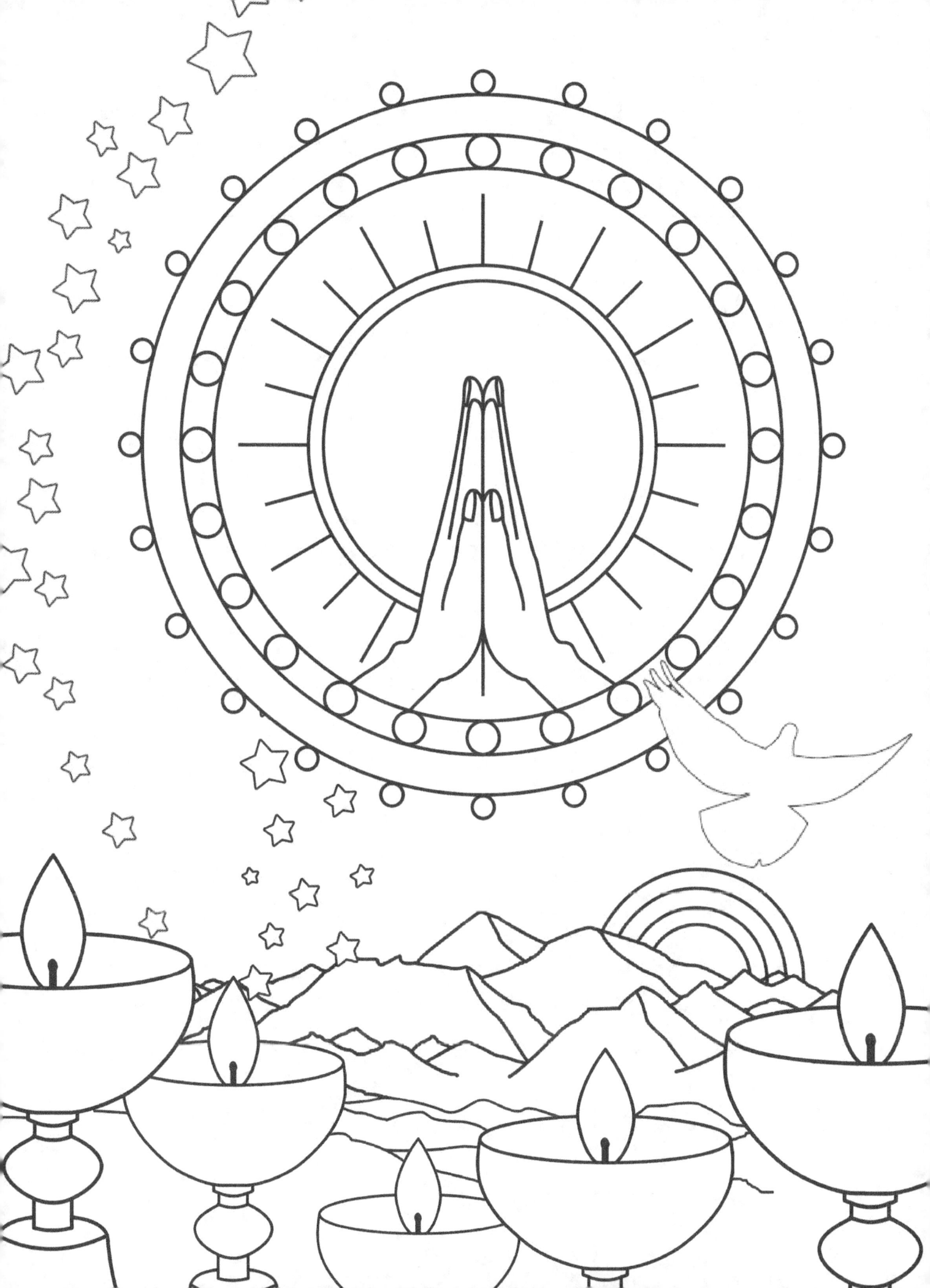

Title :

Now what comes to mind, feelings, thoughts

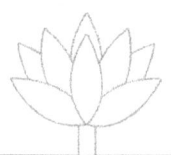

In short

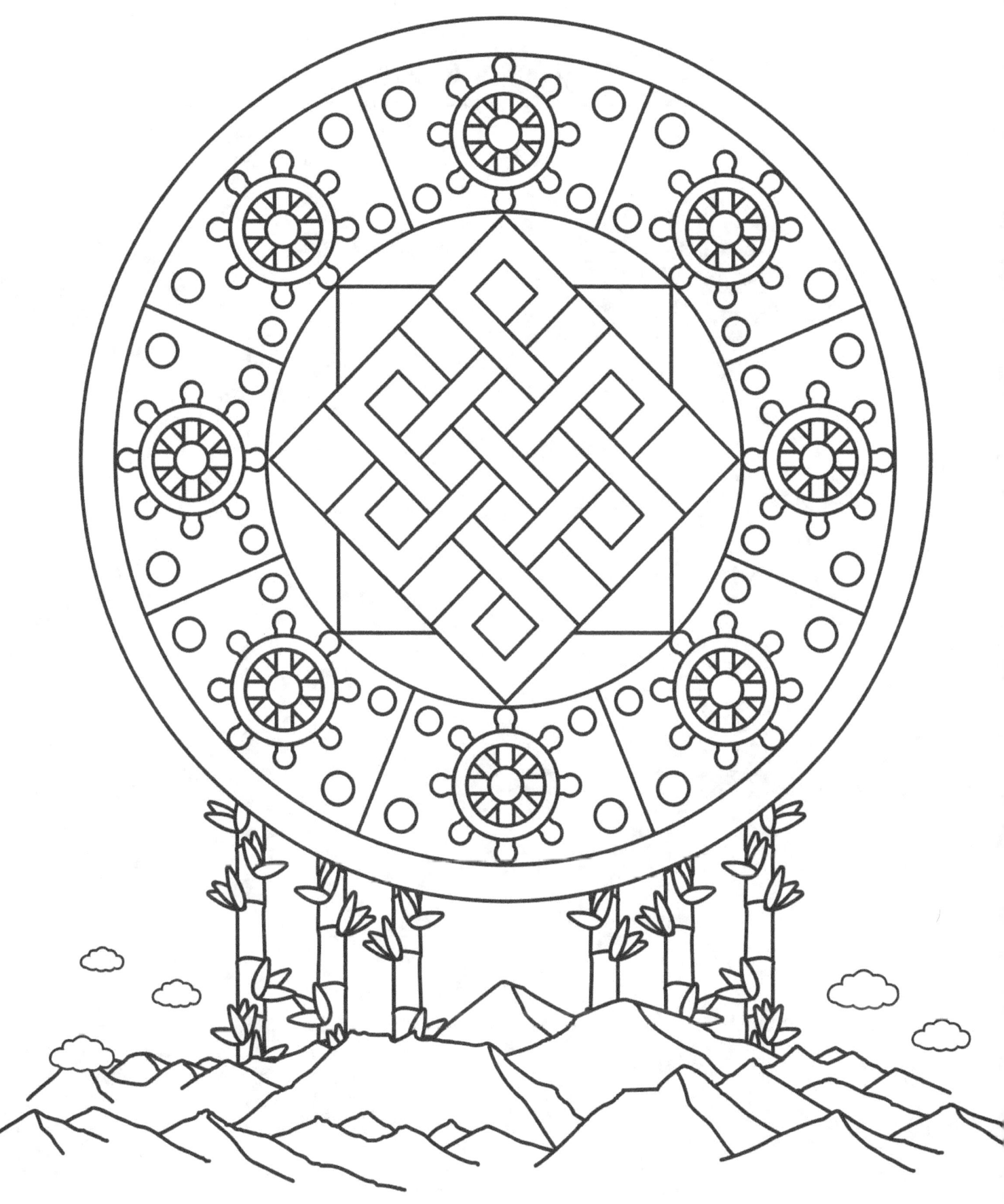

Title :

Now what comes to mind, feelings, thoughts

In short

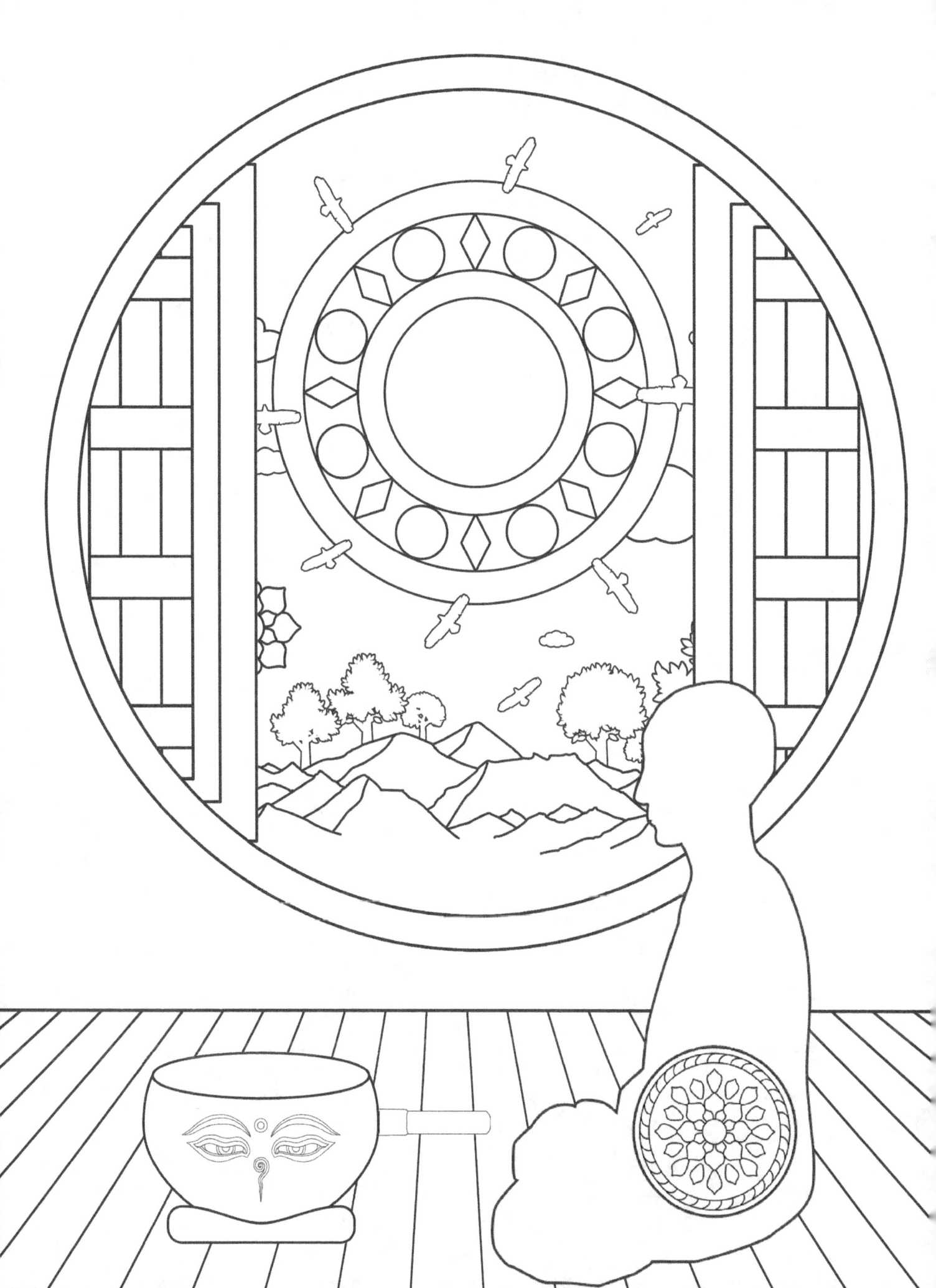

Title :

Now what comes to mind, feelings, thoughts

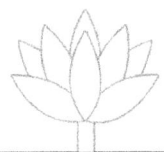

In short

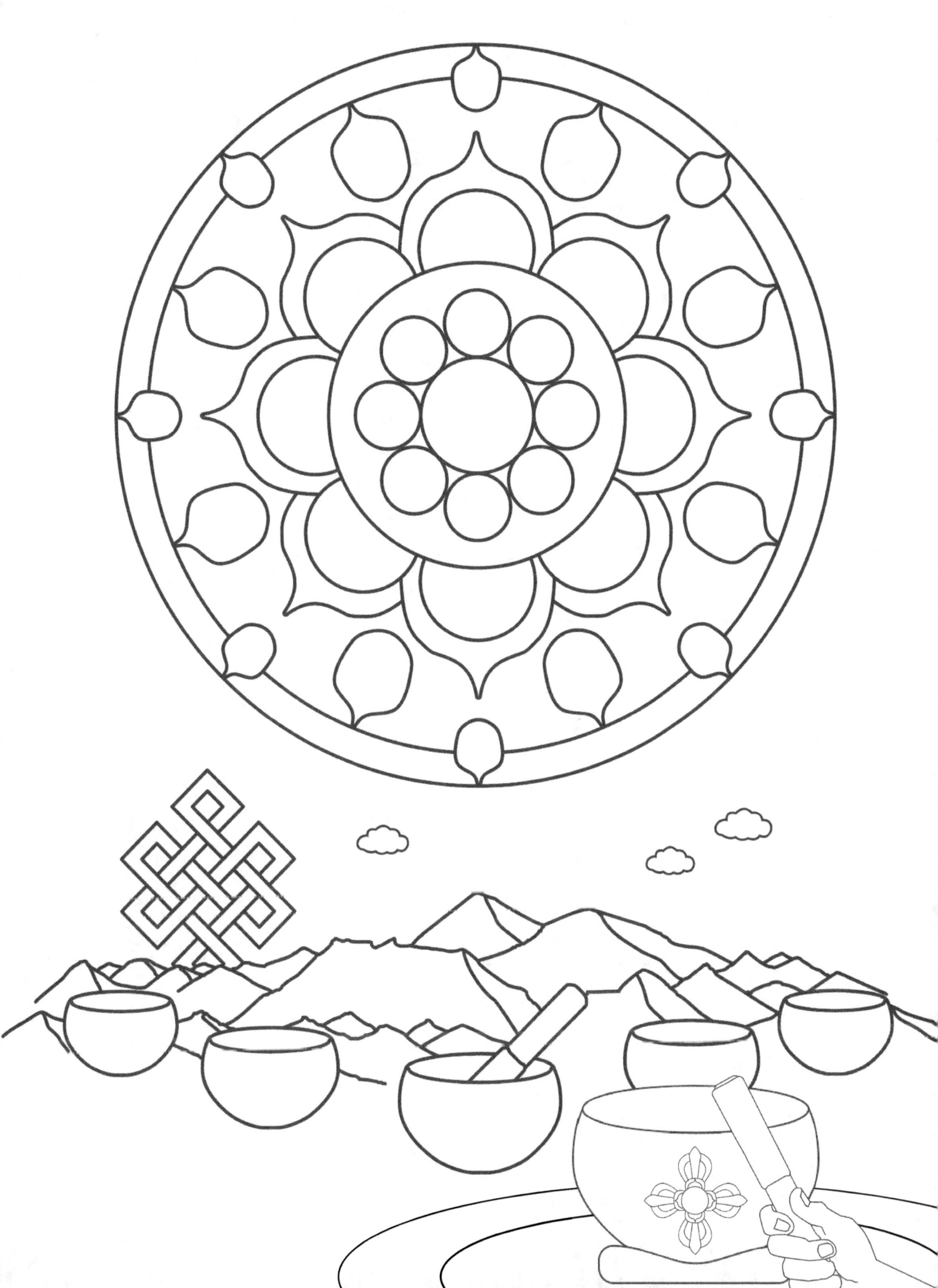

Title :

Now what comes to mind, feelings, thoughts

In short

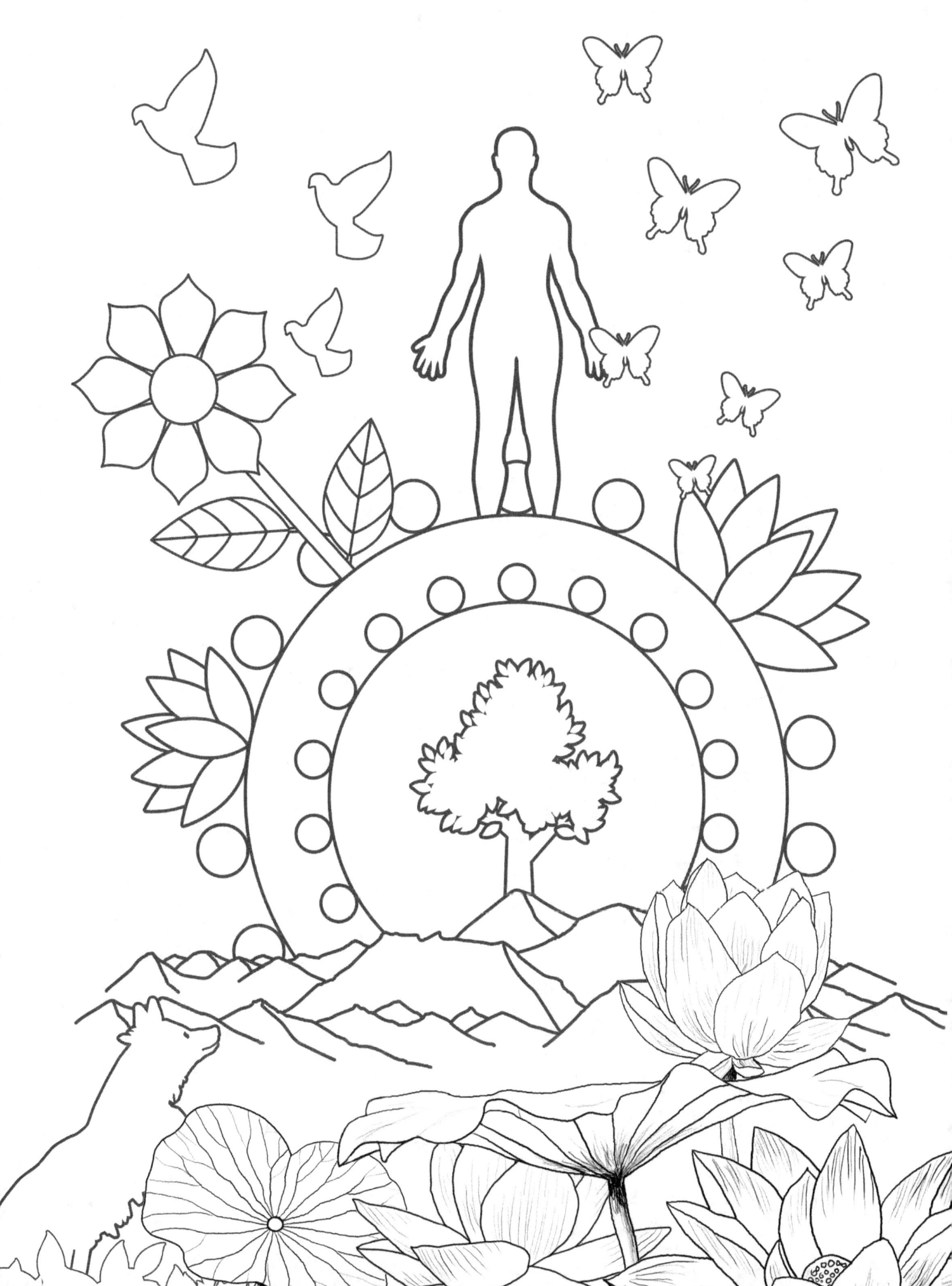

Title :

Now what comes to mind, feelings, thoughts

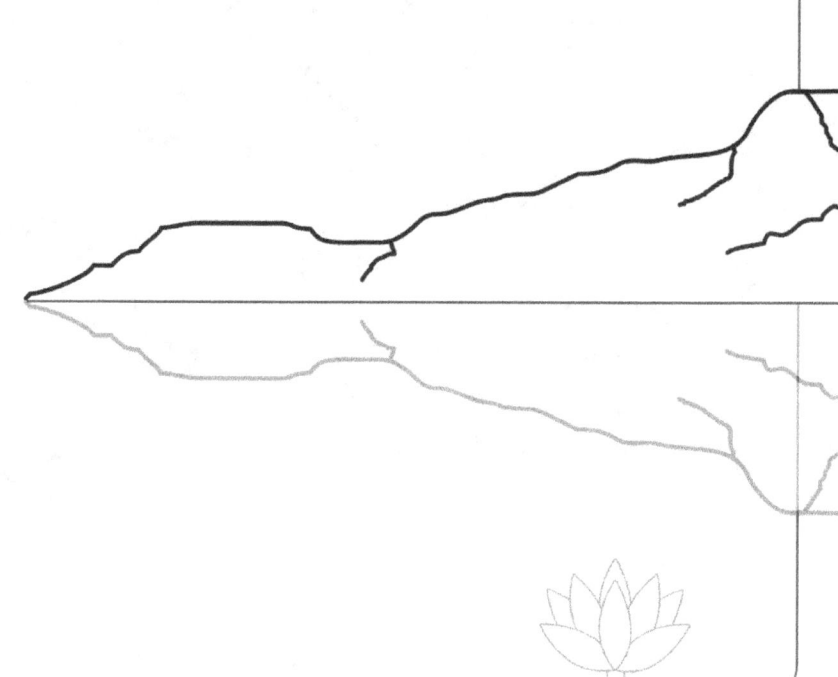

In short

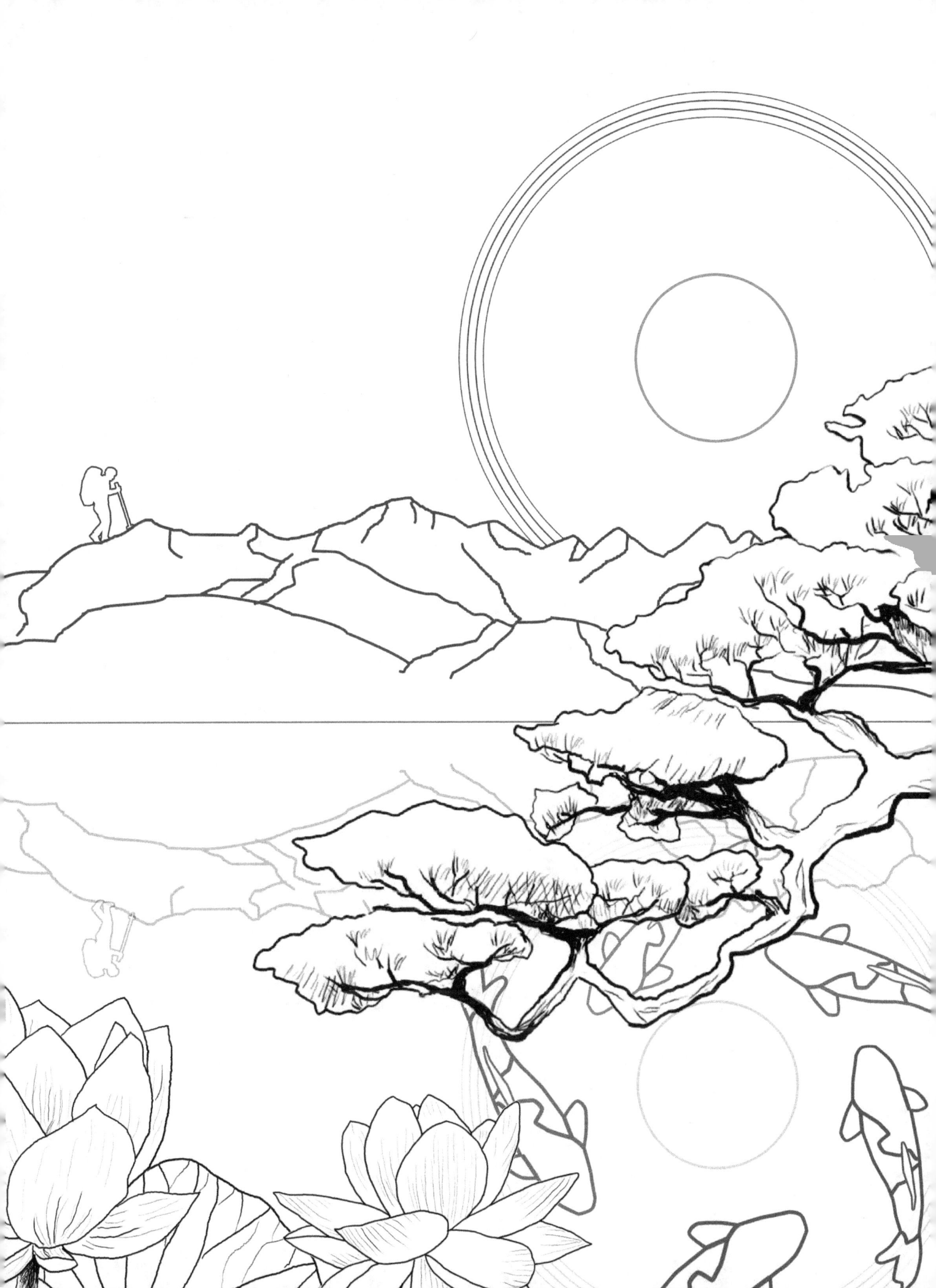

Title :

Now what comes to mind, feelings, thoughts

In short

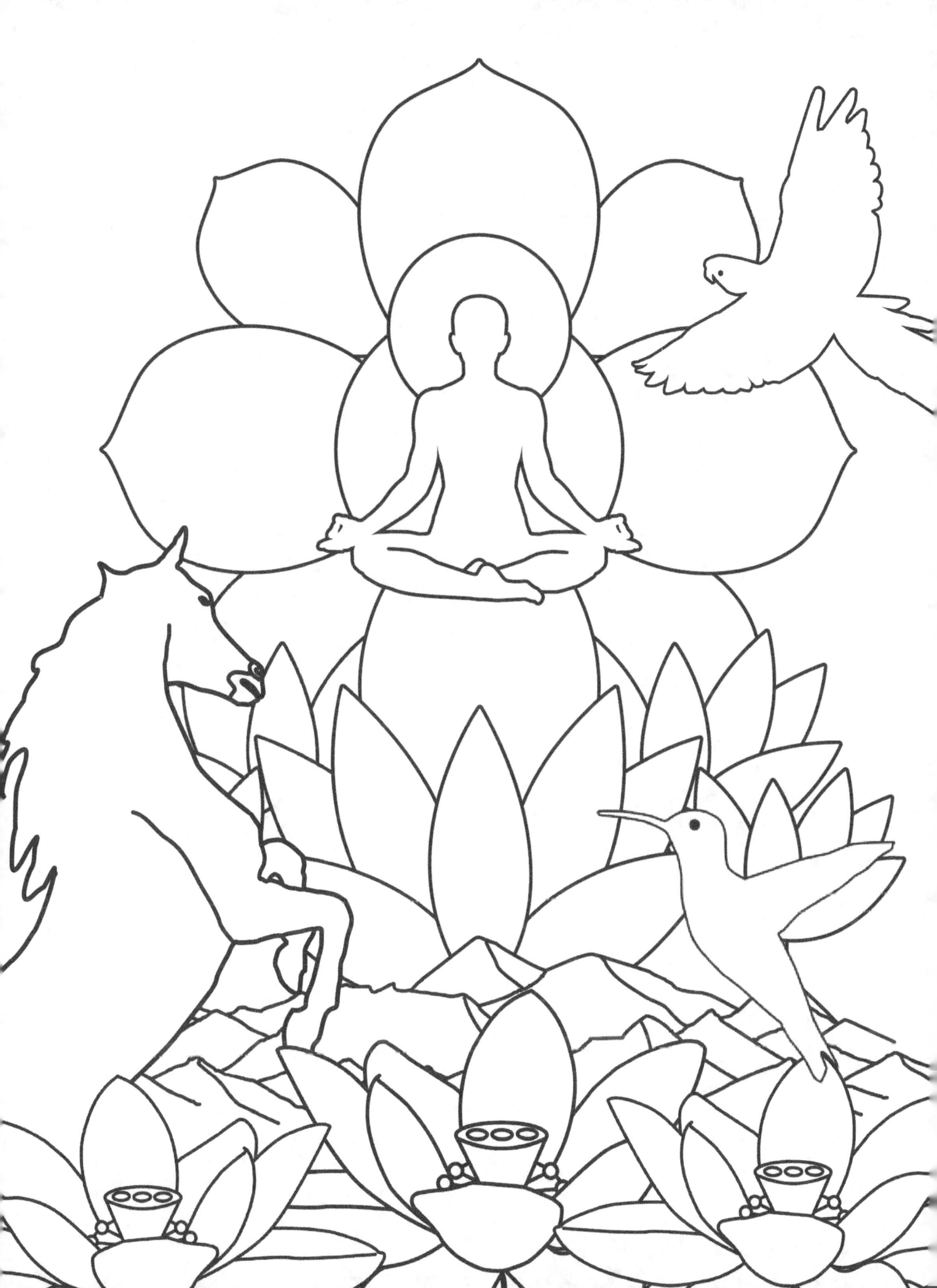

Title :

Now what comes to mind, feelings, thoughts

In short

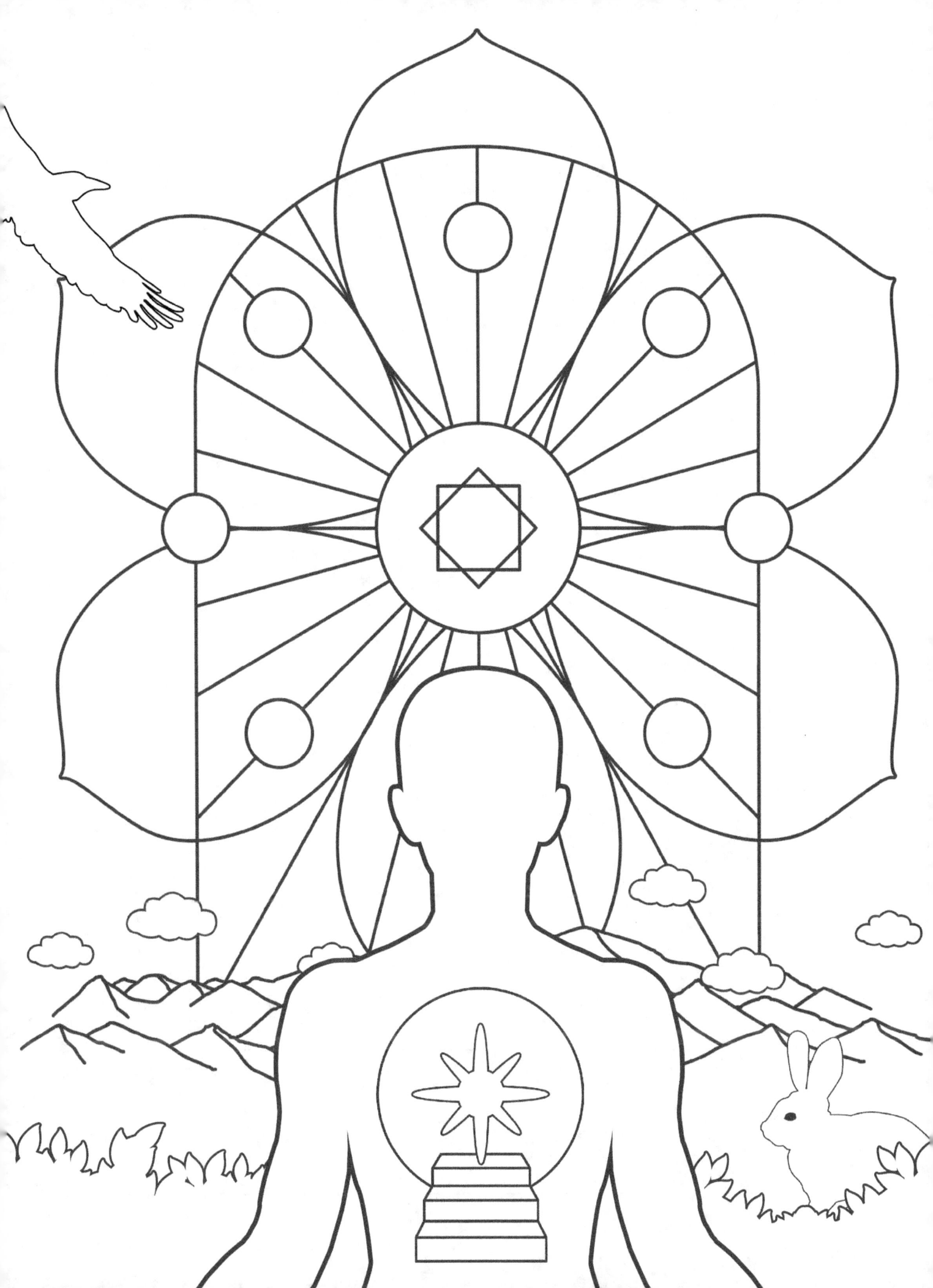

Title :

Now what comes to mind, feelings, thoughts

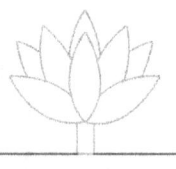

In short

Title :

Now what comes to mind, feelings, thoughts

In short

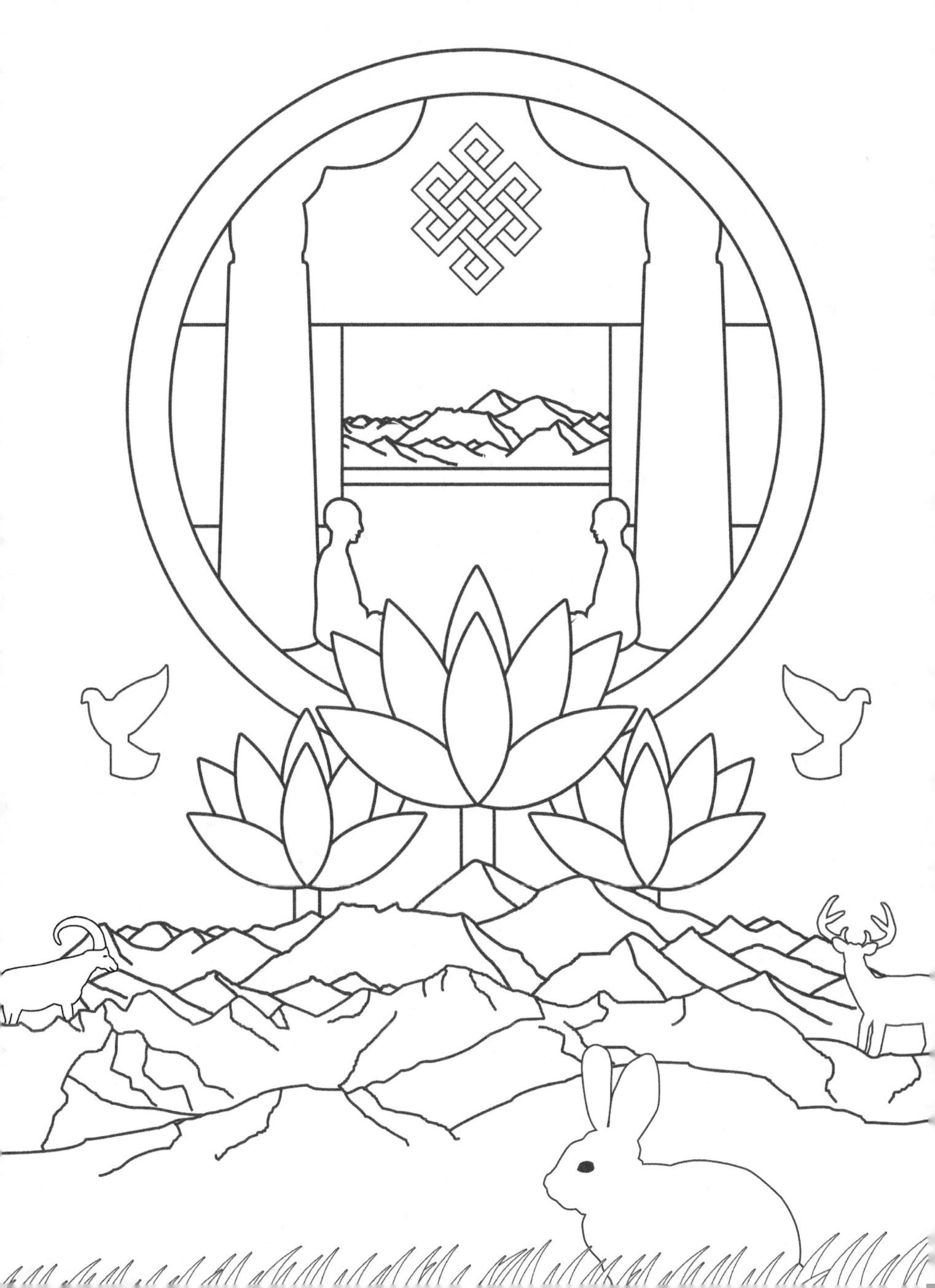

Title :

Now what comes to mind, feelings, thoughts

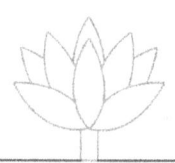

In short

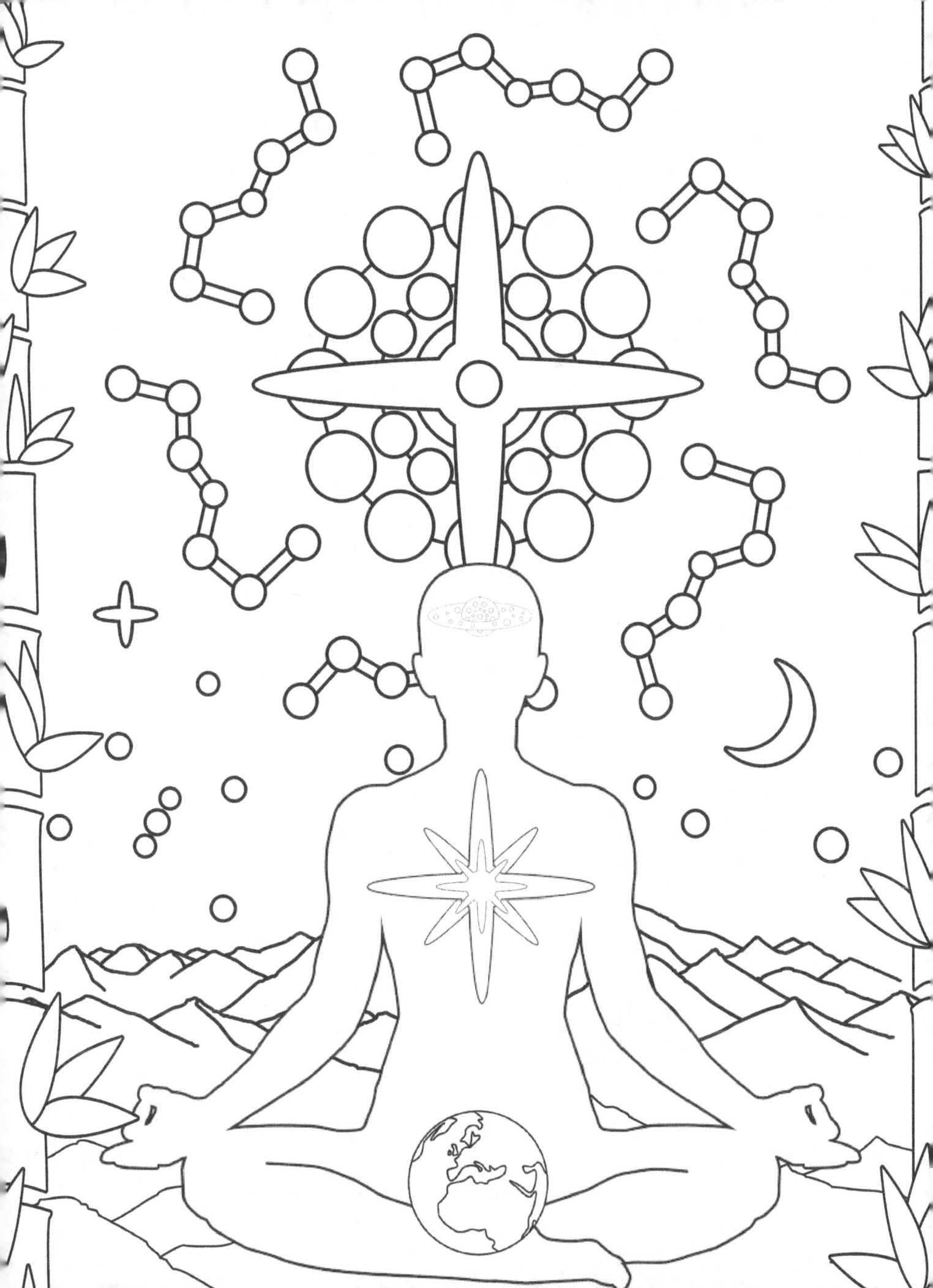

Title :

Now what comes to mind, feelings, thoughts

In short

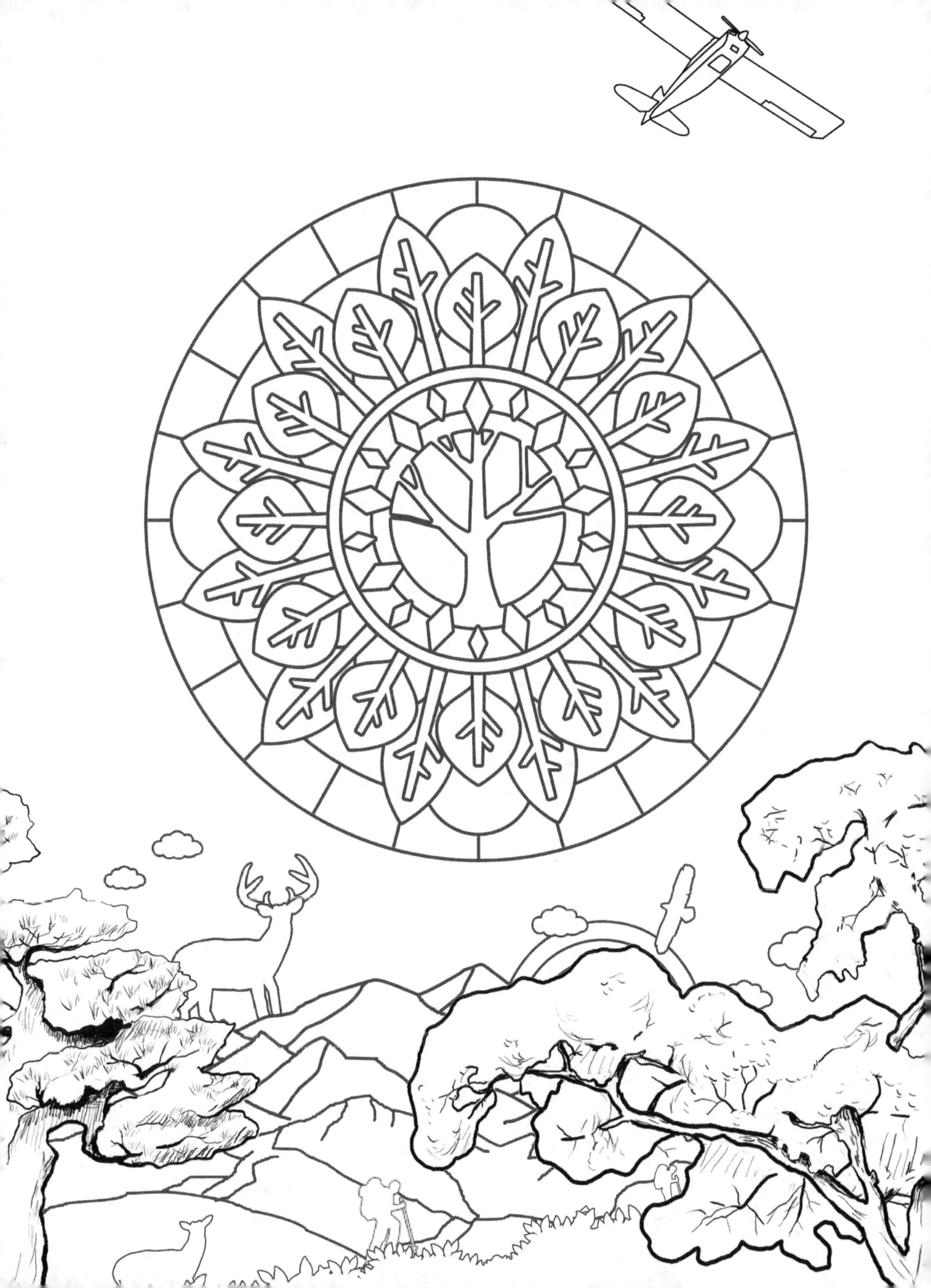

Title :

Now what comes to mind, feelings, thoughts

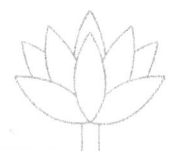

In short

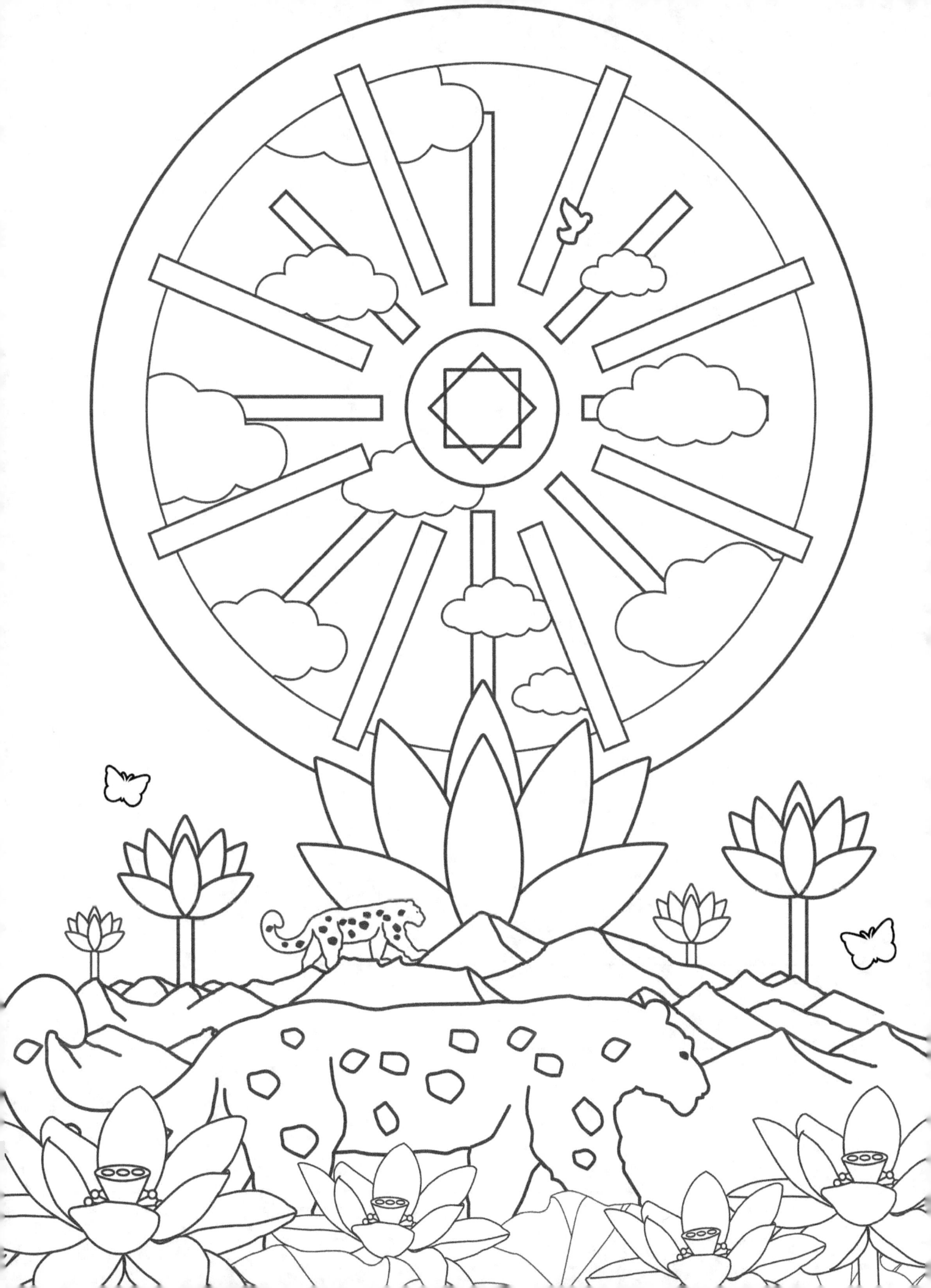

Title :

Now what comes to mind, feelings, thoughts

In short

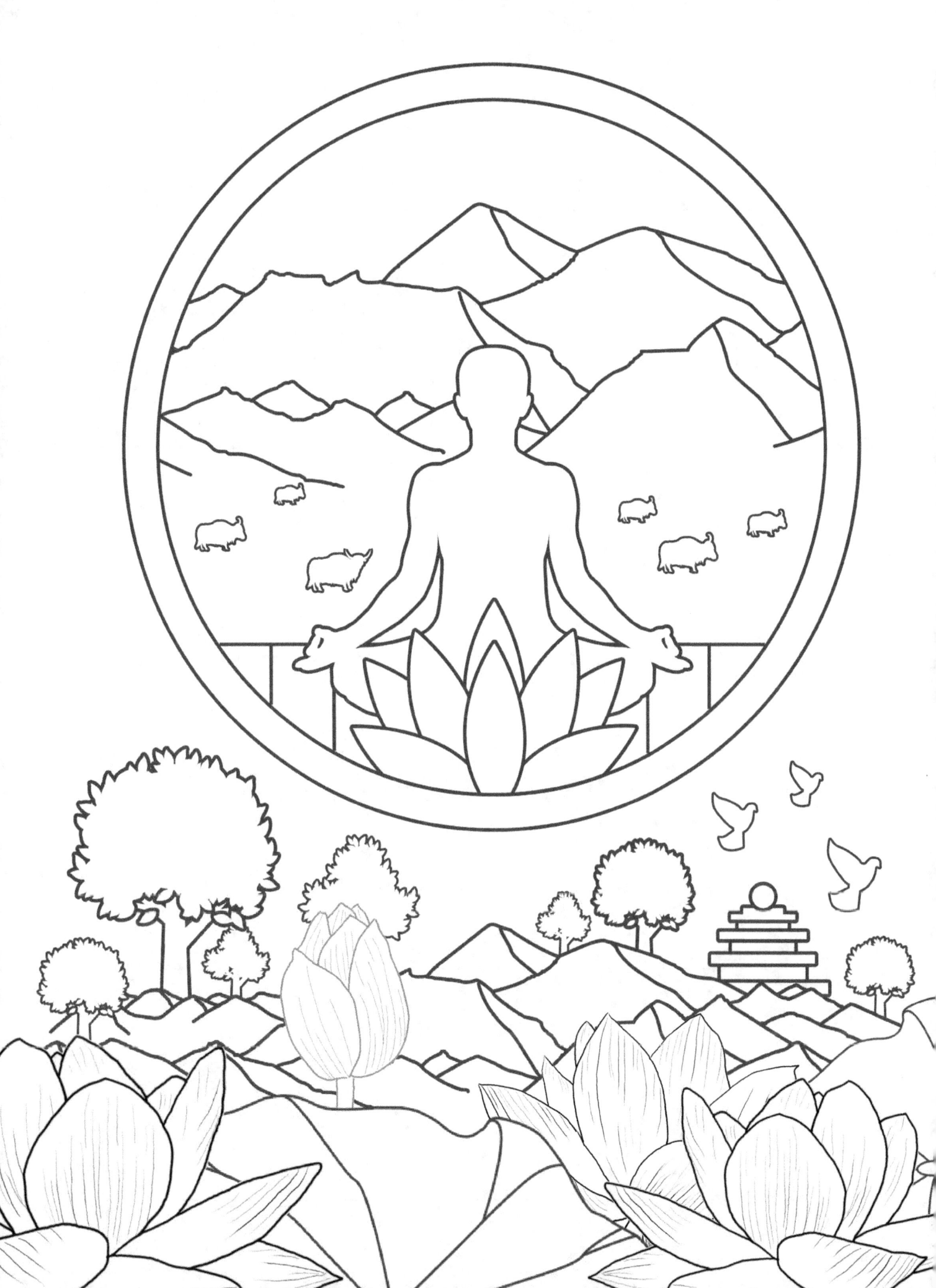

Title :

Now what comes to mind, feelings, thoughts

In short

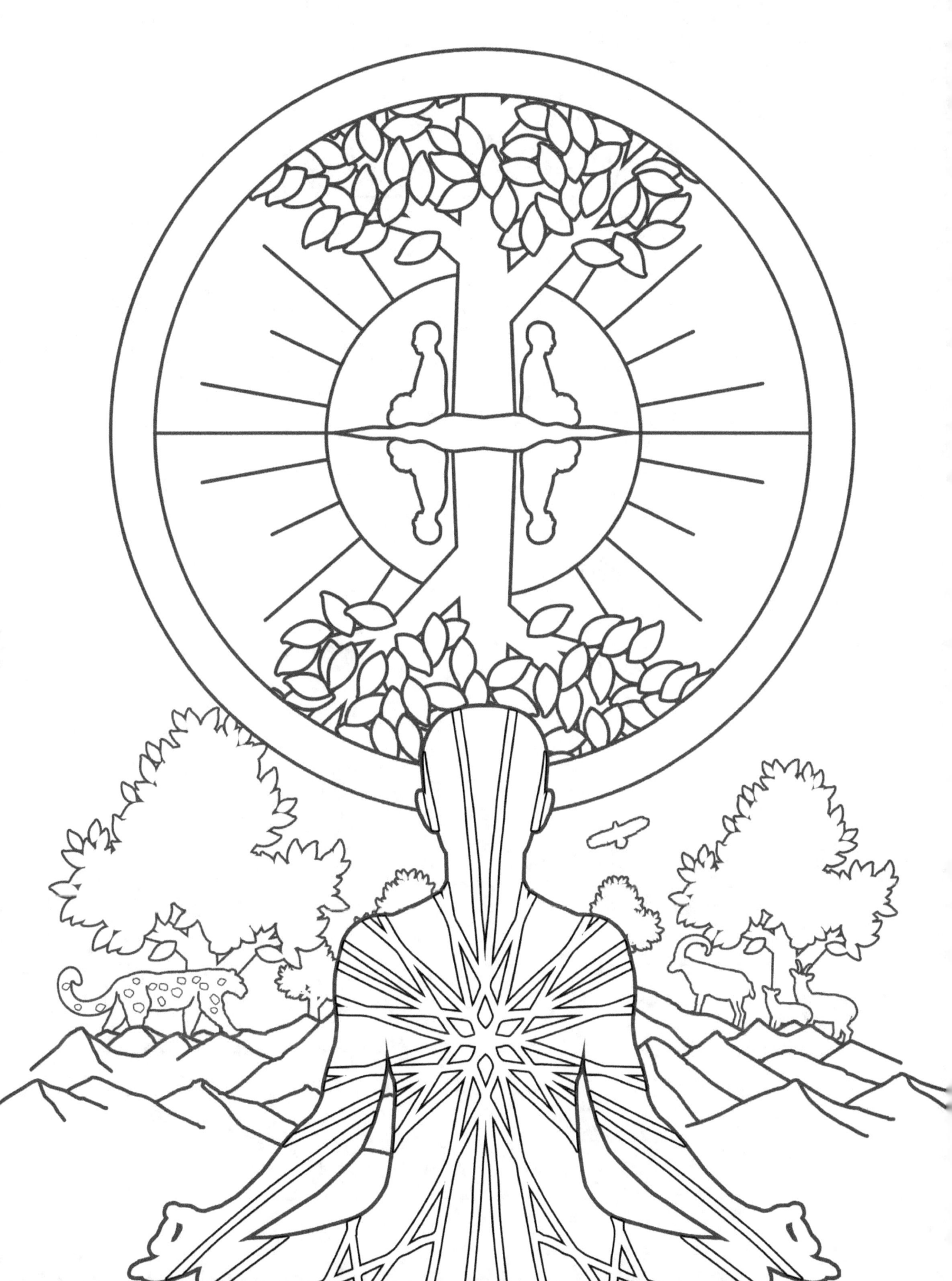

Title :

Now what comes to mind, feelings, thoughts

In short

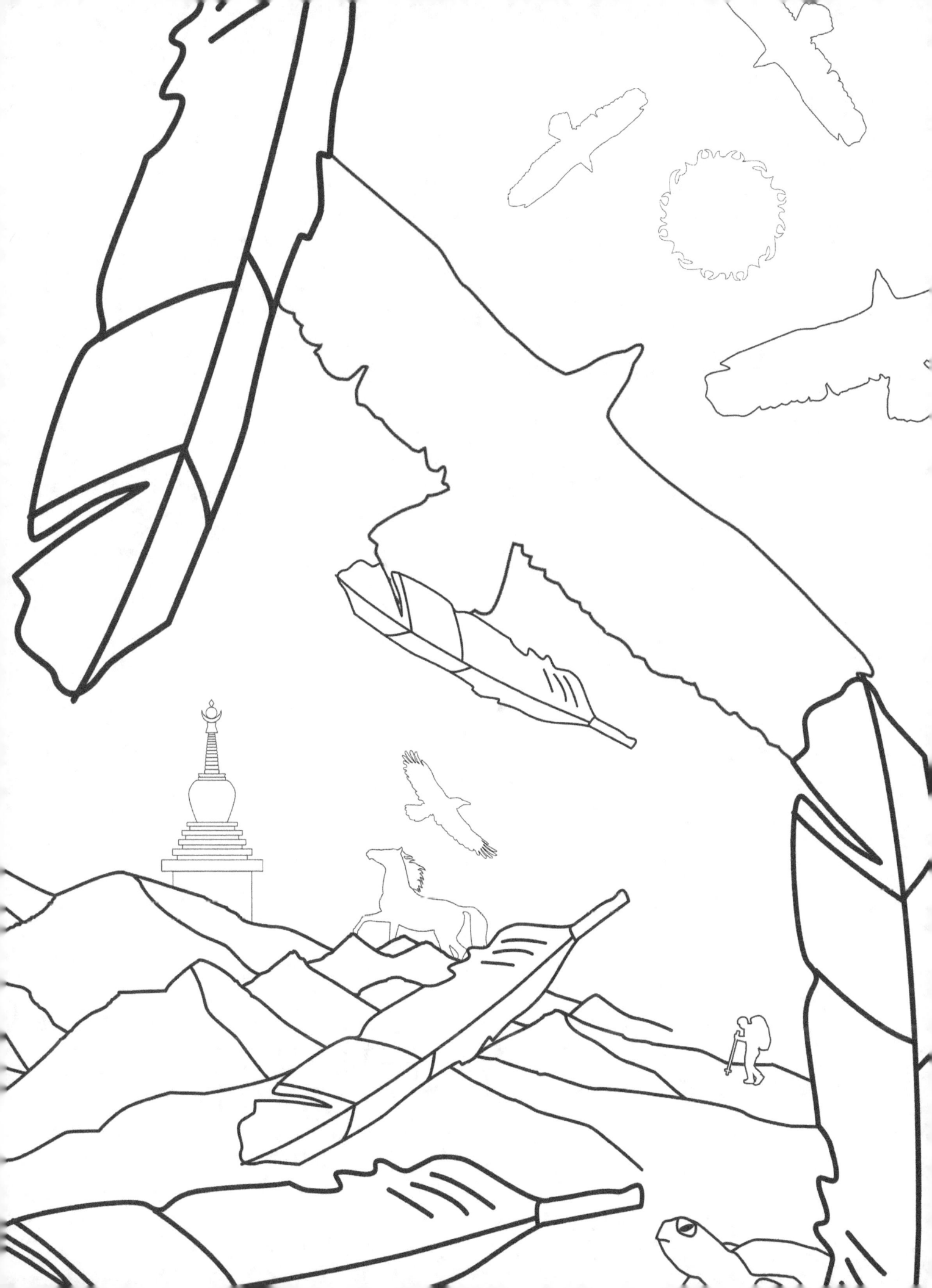

Title :

Now what comes to mind, feelings, thoughts

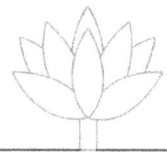

In short

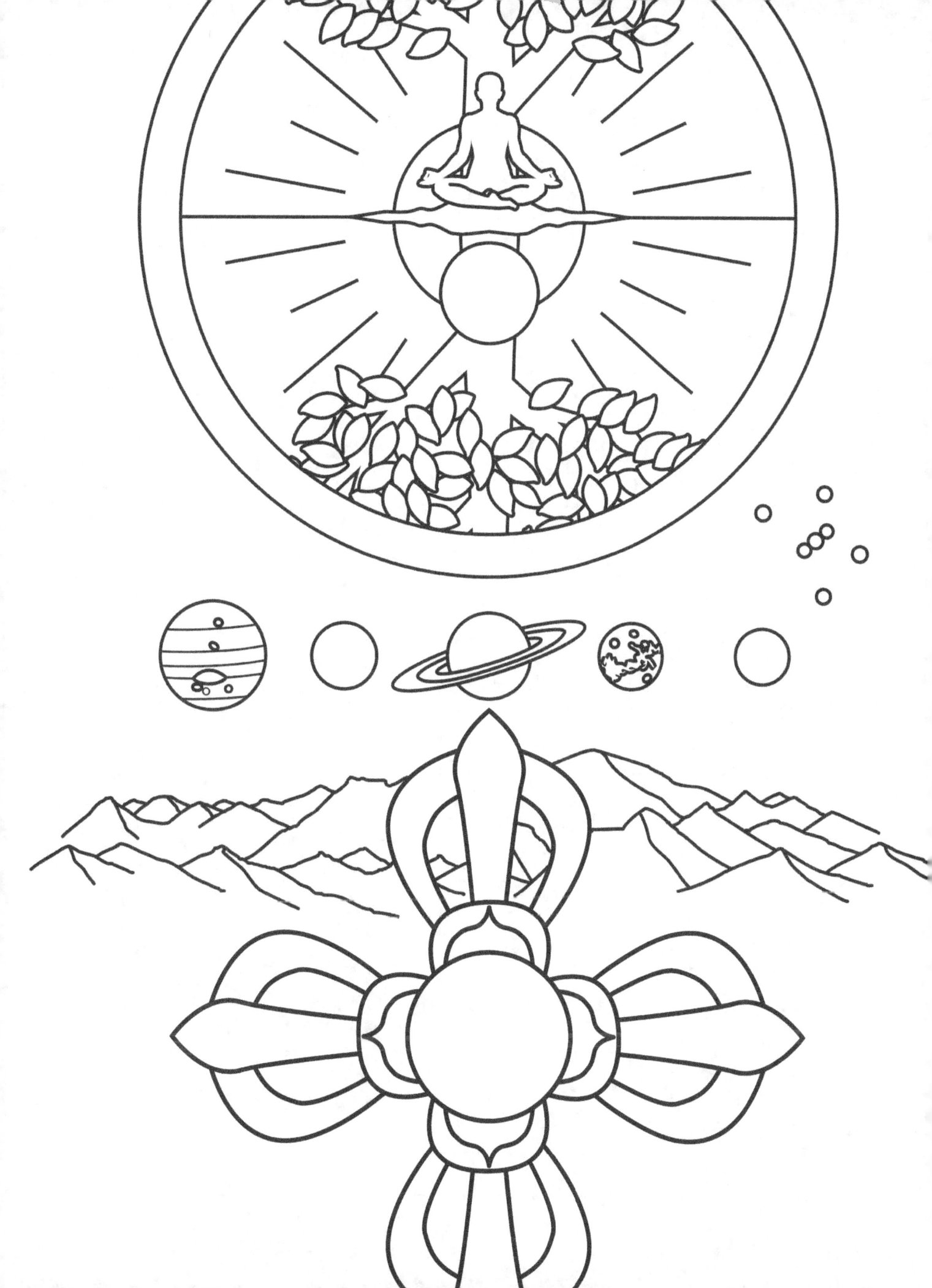

Title :

Now what comes to mind, feelings, thoughts

In short

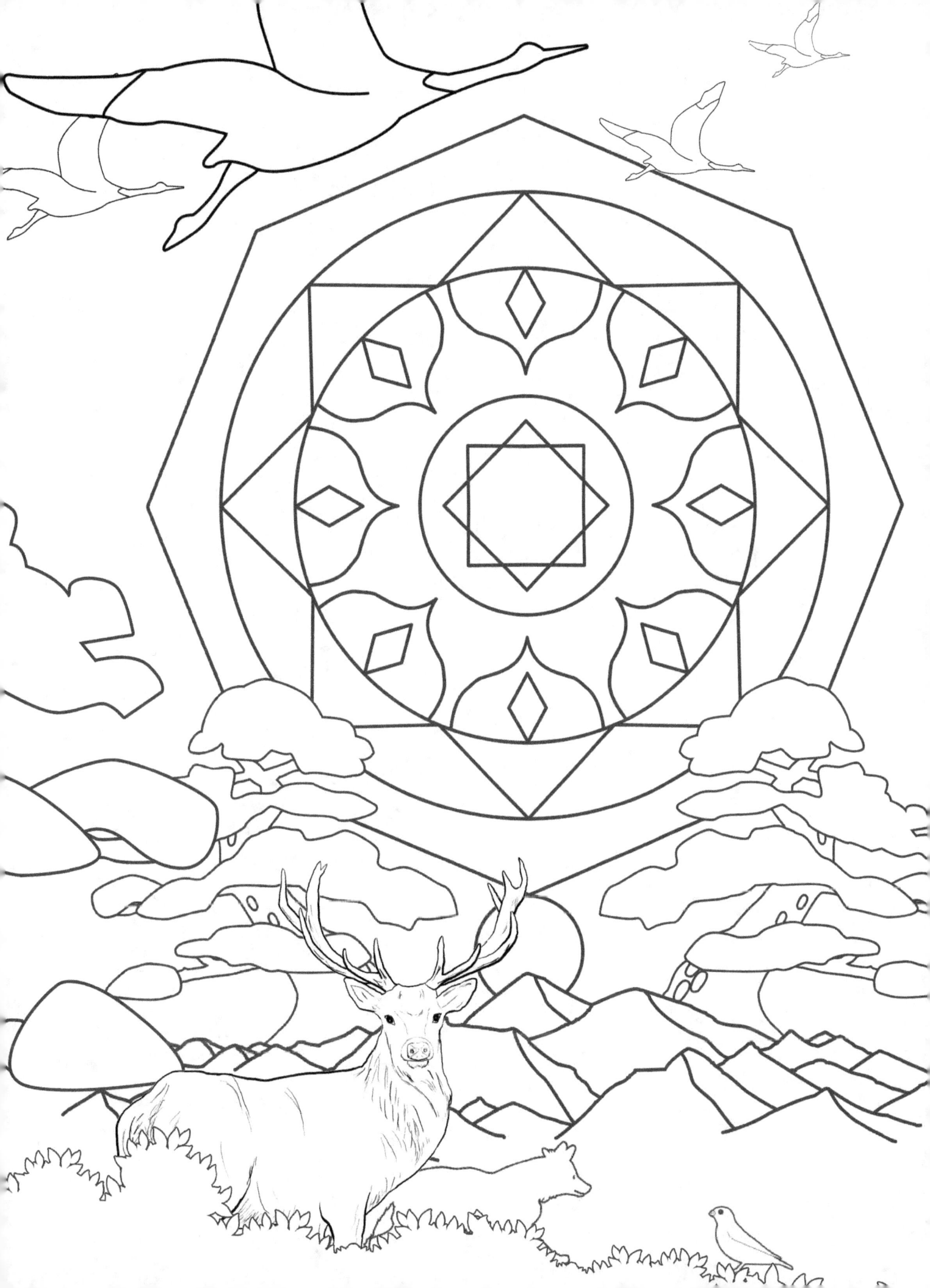

Title :

Now what comes to mind, feelings, thoughts

In short

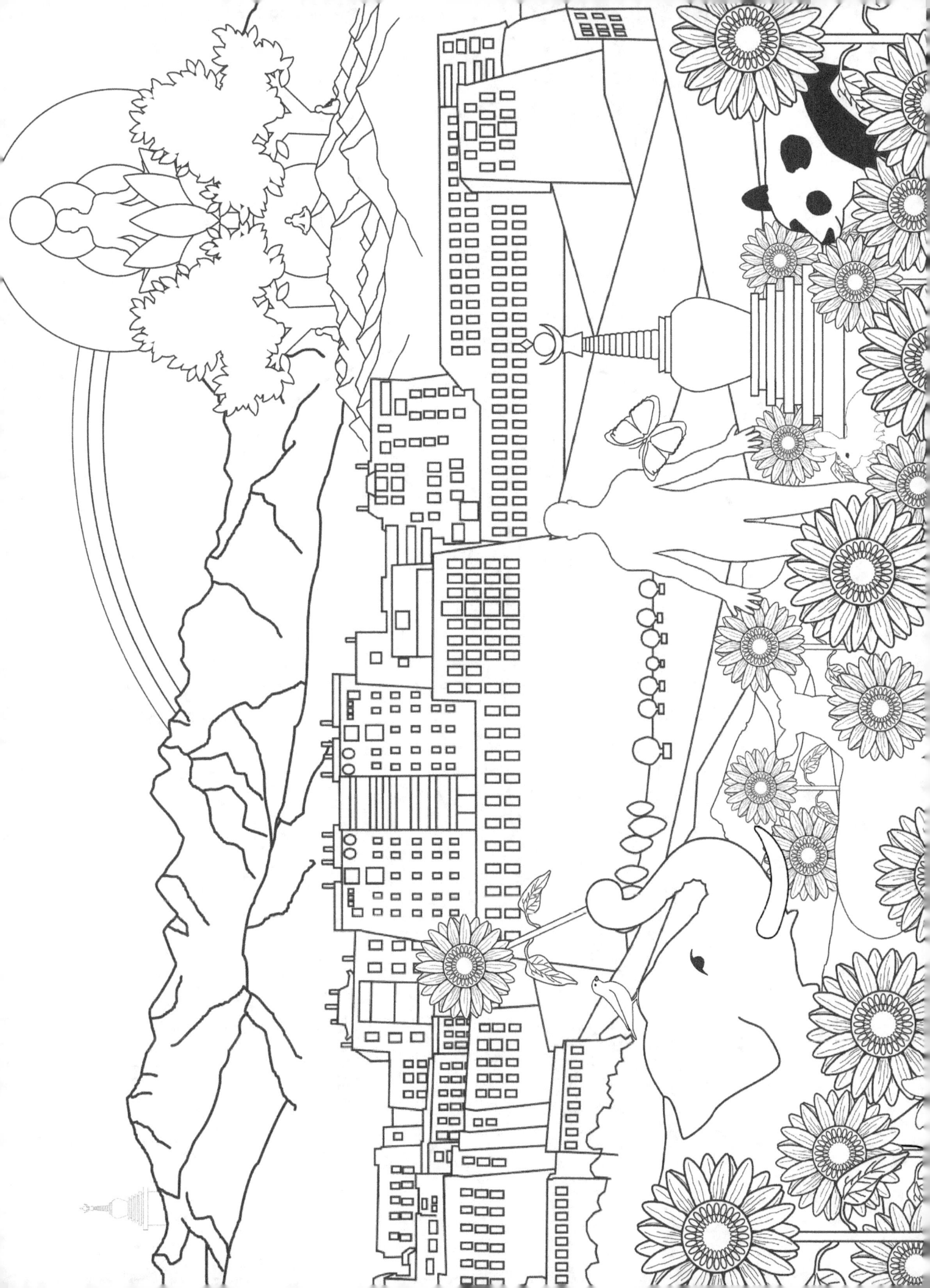

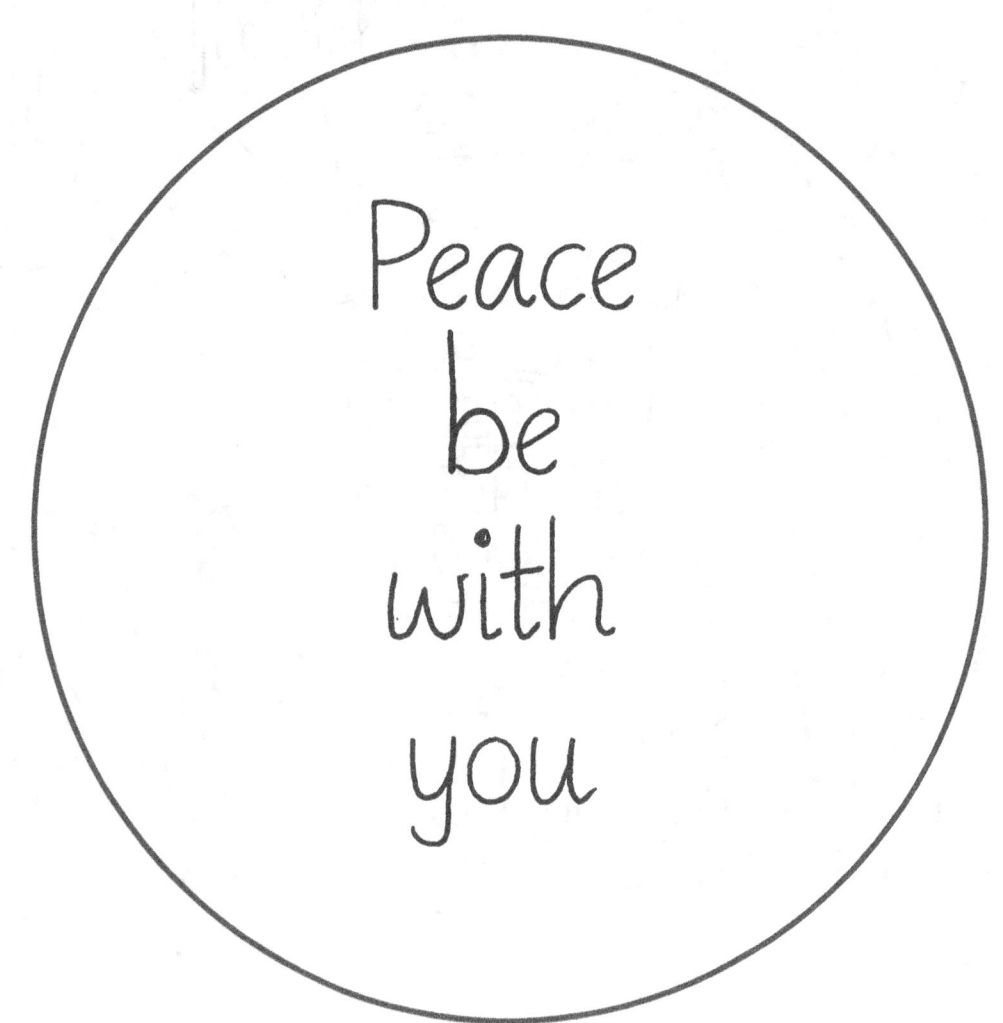